THE NEXT EXCEPTIONAL CEO

FOR BUDDING CEOs WHO HAVE A PASSION FOR THE PURSUIT OF EXCELLENCE WITHIN THEIR ORGANISATION.

RUSSELL DRISCOLL

Ark House Press
arkhousepress.com

Cataloguing in Publication Data:
Title: The Next Exceptional CEO
ISBN: 978-0-6455535-1-2 (pbk) | 978-0-6458025-0-4(ebk)
Subjects: [BUS103000] BUSINESS & ECONOMICS / Organizational Development;

Design by initiateagency.com

Albert Einstein once said,

"Life Is Like Riding a Bicycle.

To Keep Your Balance,

You Must Keep Moving"

TABLE OF CONTENTS

AUTHOR'S PREFACE

Are you inspired by all the benefits which exceptional organisations contribute? I certainly am. They produce remarkable achievements for their stakeholders, communities, country, and ocassionally even beyond their nation. They are the heartbeat of any country, providing employment, products or services, structure, reward, and community pride. Simply put, I am an advocate for sustainable organisational excellence.

I fiercely believe that this book will assist you in building success and sustainable excellence in your organisation. I wrote this book to assist senior managers (or up-and-comers) who, like me, have a passion for the pursuit of excellence within their organisation. I have written this book hoping to inspire you to excel and join the limited number of renowned and rewarded executives leading organisations that contribute to transforming their communities, nations, and beyond.

Just as in every pursuit of life, such as sport, science, literature, arts, politics, industry, and technology, we can identify individuals who excel and rise notably above their peers. So it is with organisations. Entities such as Google, Microsoft, Walt Disney, Apple, Amazon, Coca-Cola, General Electric, Mercedes Benz, World Vision, Samsung, and Singapore Airlines stand out as respected leaders within their sectors. Among all their strengths, there are four primary reasons they and many other leading organisations have achieved such success: management systems, decision making, workplace culture, and leadership. In such notable organisations, each of these four critical components is outstanding.

To gain any tangible benefit from reading this book, you will either want to develop specific core management competencies and improve your understanding of organisational performance or already possess such qualities and competencies. Hopefully, you are on a search for a holistic solution for organisational success. You will be seeking practical improvement pathways. I believe this book delivers those pathways by covering how you approach management, the quality of the daily decisions you and your management teams make, your organisation's desired culture, and you as a leader; indeed, they are the four topics of the book. The contents are the resulting accumulation of my life's work.

Early into the book, the introduction to The P9 Management Model (The Model) I developed highlights its three core and six operational elements (all beginning with a **P**). They identify the areas of responsibility that require management focus, which is essential for achieving organisational success. I explain each element's reason for existence, unique quirks, and transparent interdependency.

I give you valuable help and a sense of direction in improving your organisation's performance. As a consultant and an advisor, I have strived to understand what makes an organisation successful. I also focus on competently transferring such knowledge to others to maximise their success.

I do not intend to deliver the encyclopaedia of business; any astute senior manager will know that no single work can achieve that. Nor will reading this book guarantee you instant success. The book is not a quick-fix motivational text. I have read many of them, and they have their place, but their contents are not for the reader I seek. And to conclude on what this book does not deliver, I will point out that it does not attempt to be an exhaustive work on any topic. To achieve that, I recommend you consider undertaking formal studies, perhaps a master's degree in whatever area interests you (which this book covers). One book does not make us an expert; this only happens when one has a significant measure of knowledge and experience.

Still, by applying the contents of this book, I intend the following:

1. You can gain an alternative view of your organisation that will stretch your thinking and change your management approach
2. To introduce you to The P9 Management Model, a holistic method of structural assistance tools and philosophies
3. To enable you to focus on the detail and value of each **P** element of your organisation (you will soon understand this jargon)
4. To encourage you to apply the book's contents fully and use it to contribute towards building your organisation's sustainable excellence
5. Provide you and your critical management teams with a powerfully insightful decision-making process
6. To help you to develop an organisational-wide culture that will become the envy of your competitors
7. To assist you in becoming ***the best you*** possible

I have a passion for successful organisations and an ongoing desire to share my knowledge and experience. So, I hope you find the contents of this book easy to read, easy to understand and most importantly, easy to apply. Ultimately, I hope it challenges you and that you might consider it sufficiently worthy of becoming a benchmark reference guide in your ongoing pursuit of excellence.

Finally, this book is not an exclusive academic work. Instead, it is an informal management guidebook. I desire to share critical organisational success factors without turning the book into Tolstoy's *War and Peace*. Writing this book has, in particular, made me focus on each **P** element with greater clarity and expression. I thought I was sufficient in being across each area and in my ability to share its detail and importance. But the voyage has produced more than one surprise, which has humbled and encouraged me; so, the personal journey continues for both myself and, hopefully, you.

INTRODUCTION

What is Organisational Success? The answer to this question is essential information. It is the core intent of this book. *Why would you want to read chapter after chapter of content that either did not address or deliver the operational value of a part of the book's subtitled keywords, '**The Pursuit Of Excellence Within Their Organisation**'?*

While success is somewhat subjective and therefore open to numerous interpretations, for clarity's sake, I agree with the definition of success as being ***'the favourable or prosperous outcome of attempts or endeavours; the accomplishment of one's goals'***[1]. This definition is as true for an organisation as for an individual. Specifically, with this definition of success, I now encourage you to judge the impacting value of the subsequent chapters. While I have spent considerable time coaching and mentoring individuals to pursue personal fulfilment, this book mainly focuses on fulfilling your organisation's potential.

Suppose you have recently become responsible for an entire organisation, or a significant part thereof, that is nowhere near its potential. This book will provide considerably more than a skeleton approach to performance improvement.

It will walk you through each **P** element with sufficient detail and time to appreciate its contribution to your organisation's success. Further, it will allow you to develop and refine your opinion and

1 Succcess | Dictionary.com - https://www.dictionary.com/browse/successes

attitude towards each element. Before you begin this book, I strongly recommend you grab a notebook (paper or electronic; your choice) and be prepared to journal through each chapter recording your thoughts, reactions, responses, questions, doubts, and personal applications. Hopefully, you will experience a few light bulb moments that make your time investment wholly worthwhile.

Throughout the book, I have posed reader's questions that I encourage you to consider, meditate on, and answer in your notes. These questions will always begin with a '**R.Q.**'; the text will be in *italics* followed by '***W.I.D.***', meaning **Write It Down**.

This book is not a 'read it and leave it' text. It intends to broaden your views and firm your convictions on how an organisation of excellence looks. Your thoughts, questions, and opinions are essential ingredients. Neither is it the book you can open on any page, immediately grab a concept from, and then think you understand The Model's value. Guided by its careful' foundation-up through each level' styled crafting, step by step, you will climb through each critical component, optimising your ability to appreciate (thoroughly) the importance and value of its game-changing intent.

You will undoubtedly walk away with a greater capacity to effectively discuss organisational success. Anyone who has completed an MBA from a credible institution will tell you that such a course aims to provide the participant with a universal approach to management. You learn critical analysis; that is, to question the information presented to you. It teaches you to fully understand and apply the differences between data, information, and knowledge. It also improves your ability to manage multiple and often competing forces within your organisation.

You might consider that this book builds on the principles and contents of an MBA course. It delivers a sensible and considered approach to extraordinary holistic management, the type of management that takes an organisation that could otherwise remain average and turns it into the exceptional. Most readers will already be part of an organisation's management team and will use this book to improve the operational aspects they are responsible for. However, if undertaking a start-up, the contents will be an excellent roadmap to strategically fulfilling your objectives.

WHAT IS ORGANISATIONAL PERFORMANCE?

You tell me.

What? You say.

Why not, I say.

Why would your opinion be of less value than the raft of views on offer by numerous academics, authors, and commentators that (by any reasonable assessment) reveals a considerable variance of theories? The fact is that the term Organisational Performance can be subjective and elusive.

I first heard of the term used by a global fuel company in the late 1970s (yes, I'm that old), referring to an organisation's means and ends. However, I'm sure there must have been at least some conceptual discussion of the topic in the early seasons of the Industrial Revolution. Researchers write that during the 1980s, management consultants defined organisational performance as *"the extent to which an organisation, as a social system, could value both its means and its ends"*[2].

In this millennium, academics and specialist consulting firms have undertaken extensive research to understand the intricacies of this topic. It now seems popular to describe Organisational

2 Sociology Research | Organizations as Social Structures - Sociology of Organizations - iResearchNet

Performance as two broad measures. Firstly, economic performance measures financial and market outcomes by assessing profits, sales, growth, return on investment, and other financial metrics. The second scope of measurement is less tangible. It relates to operational performance, focusing on the visible indices such as the organisation's social capital, customer satisfaction and loyalty, and competitive edge resulting from resources and capabilities.

The real-world measurement of Organisational Performance also varies but can be categorised as **survival and growth** (meeting specified goals with continual improvement), **environment fit** (ability to achieve high productivity and employee satisfaction with minimal turnover rates and costs), and **stakeholder relevancy** (of the entire extent of their stakeholders). I have used parts of the work that CQ Net[3] (Tahir, 2020) offers to explain this topic to articulate my opinion.

When assessing the commonalities of numerous highly successful organisations, I agree with those who conclude that high organisational performance occurs when stated objectives are met with optimum resources to satisfy relevant stakeholder demands.

How is it measured?

There needs to be different measurement approaches utilised for the different levels within an organisation, individual-level, team-level and organisational level. The individual level is initially task-focused which leads to contextual and adaptive performance. However, measuring team-level performance requires a more systematic approach. This approach includes assessing team proficiency and considering team adaptability, alignment, and leadership. The organisational level is measured by focusing on the macro view of conventional financial metrics.

One other measurement view compares a single organisation to its sector cohorts. Naturally, this is the one that continually

---

3 Organisational Performance | (Tahir, 2020) - https://www.ckju.net/en/organizational-performance-what-it-is-how-to-measure-and-improve-it

attracts the attention of CEOs because it ultimately influences their reward.

So, numerous indicators measure organisational performance at different levels. The decider for your correct organisational performance measurement method needs to be the rationale you develop. This approach often evolves into a matrix of relevant data and a final index.

Application

I prefer to promote that organisational performance should be a measure of excellence. In this book's Introduction, I expressed my passion for directing you to build success and sustainable excellence in your organisation. I am convinced that your buy-in to the principles described throughout this book, and your willingness to follow them, will determine the long-term success of your organisation's future.

The P9 Management Model was (partly) developed to deliver the Think Big view of organisational performance by measuring the six operational umbrella P elements described in the next chapter. It is the global view of your organisation. Thorough assessment, using individually tailored systems specific to your organisation, that will deliver vital information to senior management, thus enabling and empowering them to identify performance outcomes and correct, where necessary, matters that need improvement. This book is an invaluable asset for those responsible for achieving sustainable excellence that ensures organisational success.

1

THE P9 MANAGEMENT MODEL

> *"a diamond discovery for senior management".*

Welcome to The P9 Management Model (The Model). The following eleven foundational description chapters deal with the structure and philosophy of The Model before advancing to the details of the other three crucial components of The Model.

Science has never been my strongest subject, but I still recognise its critical importance to my quality of life and future life. Scientists state that life consists of matter at its most fundamental level. Matter is any substance that occupies space and has mass. Elements are unique forms of matter with specific chemical and physical properties that cannot be broken down into smaller substances by ordinary chemical reactions[4].

The Periodic Table identifies over 100 elements structured in 18 groups. I remain unsuccessful at memorising them.

---

4 Matter | Nigerian Scholars - https://nigerianscholars.com/tutorials/chemical-foundation-of-life/the-building-blocks-of-life/

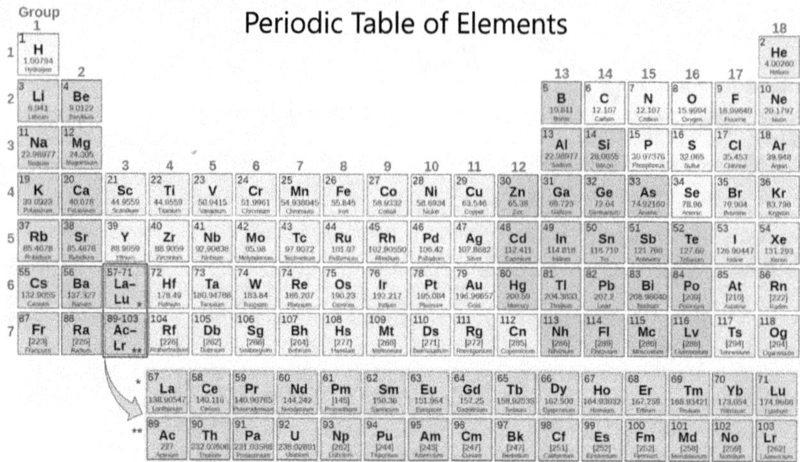

Periodic Table of Elements
Group
H He
Li Be B C N O F Ne
Na Mg Al Si P S Cl Ar
K Ca Sc Ti V Cr Mn Fe Co Ni Cu Zn Ga Ge As Se Br Kr
Rb Sr Y Zr Nb Mo Tc Ru Rh Pd Ag Cd In Sn Sb Te I Xe
Cs Ba La-Lu Hf Ta W Re Os Ir Pt Au Hg Tl Pb Bi Po At Rn
Fr Ra Ac-Lr Rf Db Sg Bh Hs Mt Ds Rg Cn Nh Fl Mc Lv Ts Og
La Ce Pr Nd Pm Sm Eu Gd Tb Dy Ho Er Tm Yb Lu
Ac Th Pa U Np Pu Am Cm Bk Cf Es Fm Md No Lr

However, I applied the same methodology of identifying and grouping organisational elements when developing The P9 Management Model to share what I learned about highly successful organisations. Fortunately, my research into the elements of an organisation resulted in identifying only nine. Any manager can remember nine elements, especially when understanding them and learning how quality management of their interrelational impacts can potentially change their world.

Application

Essentially, it is about applying the principles and power of The Model to improve performance and potentially achieve organisational excellence and sustainability. It stretches you to rethink your opinions and attitudes. You become a campaigner for exceptional performance and sustainable excellence.

The Model delivers considerably more than structural frameworks, theories and recommended procedures. I will introduce you to alternative thinking, different approaches and improved core values that will create a distinctly better organisation-wide, purpose-driven and respected culture that will become the envy of your opposition.

In my Introduction, I referred to Organisational Success. Organisations, irrespective of sector, type, size, or location, consist of numerous parts and many descriptions given to such parts.

R.Q. *What automatically comes to your mind when you think of the parts of your organisation?* ***W.I.D.***

Business units, divisions, departments, structure, workflows, human resources, product, distribution, service delivery, marketing? This group grows into a sizable list, and each part requires attention, strategic thought, and effective management.

My experience is that most senior managers are both competent and professional. When needed, they can call on the marketplace, with no shortage of advisors and consultants to assist in these specific parts.

So, what is the problem? Why do you need another model, theory, tool or philosophy?

If you are already a highly successful and renowned organisation of excellence, then the short answer is that you don't. However, if that is not an accurate description of your organisation, then continuing to read this book could be the game-changer you need.

Since the Industrial Revolution, senior managers have continually faced greater daily workloads and a broader raft of responsibilities, pressures, and expectations. Surveys highlight that '*continuously being in demand*' places immense pressure on senior management, who are also having to ensure that their organisation (in the case of a CEO), or their 'part' of their organisation (divisional/departmental managers), continually outperforms last year's results.

Consequently, their focus must be on managing their 'part' while not ignoring the direct impact on their results by managers responsible for other 'parts'. Exceptional organisations do not have weak spots. They did not become highly successful by holding onto a small vision, having small-minded people, or tolerating underdeveloped processors. Although to varying degrees, this is still the experience of most contemporary organisations.

So, there needs to be a paradigm shift from average to exceptional. At a minimum, you need competent and professional management in each area of your organisation. Nevertheless, to achieve organisational excellence, there must be a different approach.

The Model's focus on achieving exceptional organisation-wide performance majors on the following factors:

1. Managers acknowledge and understand that the 9P's umbrella elements' balanced position and prominence indisputably affect their organisation's performance and then apply The Model's principles and philosophies
2. It will measurably improve the quality of management decision-making
3. Senior managers will not just focus on their various 'parts' but also choose to be continuously mindful of the broader nine umbrella elements of their entire organisation while developing The P9 Cohesive Management Culture
4. Quality Leadership

What are the 9Ps?

Each 'P' is a descriptive umbrella title that heads up critically specific areas of responsibility within your organisation. The Model refers to these as elements, an essential or characteristic part of something abstract.

The 9Ps of organisations are Purpose, People, Processes (the three core elements), Protection & Policies, Practices & Performance, Product & Promotion (the six operational elements; more on the correctness of these later). The academic world of business is full of opinions on critical components of organisations, many of which I have previously studied. My goal in developing The Model was clear, help senior management achieve organisational-wide excellence by providing a practical yet highly effective tool that empowers managers to identify, measure, and resolve issues that negatively influence performance. I wrote this book with the predetermined view that you will either already agree with those 9Ps or at least be willing to be convinced.

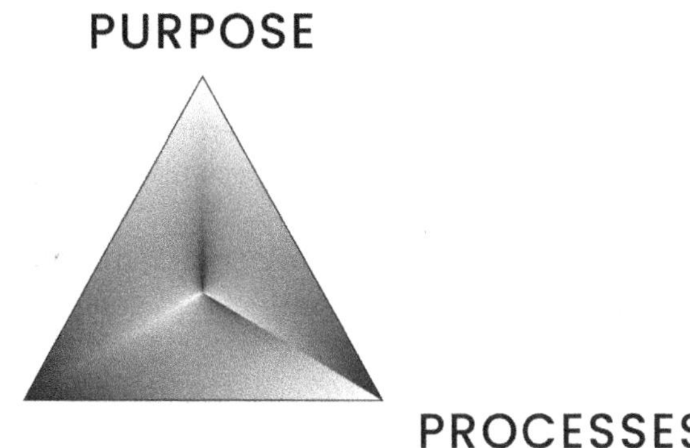

I explain why each element is critical to performance outcomes throughout the book. This book requires you to think carefully about your estimate concerning each P's place, priority, and performance within your organisation, compared to the other Ps.

The book is relevant to all organisations, no matter their size, sector, or history. Each 'P' is present in every organisation.

Each one needs to be fully understood to fulfil its role within your organisation. Each 'P' requires acknowledgement, respect, strategic consideration, intentionality, committed investment, and comprehensive management.

Having a respectful understanding of each 'P' is logically essential. The next level is a differentiator; you will possess the knowledge and ability to quickly recall how they impact each other, together with skills and tools to identify and resolve negative performance issues.

From where did The P9 Management Model come?

Like many before, I have spent years observing, researching, and documenting commonalities that make specific organisations highly successful. This effort resulted in gathering volumes of notes, images, recordings, clippings, and shelves of reference books.

The challenge I faced (and that faces almost every senior manager) was threefold:

- Compacting all that information into a usable vehicle
- Concisely articulating what I had learnt
- To reach organisational excellence, I would have to develop methods to convincingly demonstrate that applying such knowledge will lead to successfully implementing solutions

I began placing the various collected items into separately named folders, but the number of folders was still confronting, with each folder being too voluminous. Over time, I repositioned those folders into a logical hierarchical structure of folders, but still, the number was considerable and lacked relational insights.

After a period of reflection, I realised I had forgotten some valuable lessons from earlier experiences of learning how to memorise required information. So, I wanted to find a simple way to remember each critical element and create a descriptive umbrella approach.

The rest was relatively easy, as **the unquestionable factor I discovered** in every highly successful organisation was their **purpose**-driven approach. It was their ***Why*** umbrella! The cornerstone of everything else. Next, their **people** provided their ***What*** element; even if through robotics, whatever was needed to be done was executed and managed by people. That left their ***How*** factor, the how everything was done, which I recognised as the **Processes** umbrella.

When it comes to organisational success, these three umbrella elements of **Purpose**, **People** and **Processes** are the primary (core) elements. They provide the foundational strength and critically important interrelational location of each core area of management. They indeed are the Why, What & How elements of every organisation.

The diagrammatic layout of The Model requires the user to follow it in the anticlockwise direction. It is the correct and pragmatically logical procedural pathway of progress. It ensures the outcomes of exceptional organisational performance and essential foundations for sustainable excellence when carefully followed and implemented.

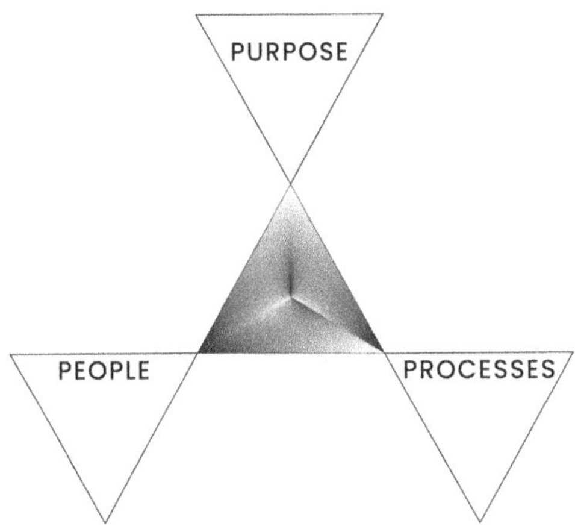

A worthy & defined Purpose delivered by valued **People** utilising highly developed **Processes** = organisational success leading to sustainable excellence! When speaking on organisational excellence, this is one of my key mantras.

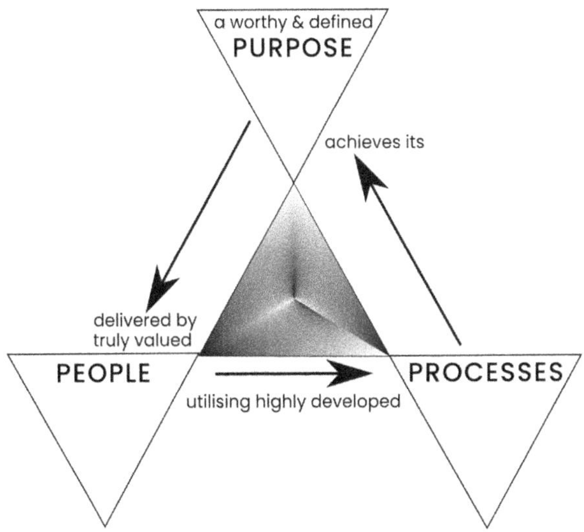

Everything else (covered by the remaining six P's) flows from these three. Having the three core elements all begin with a 'P', I started the process of grouping every aspect and activity present within any organisation, recognising that some or many activities would be present in more than one group. Again, minimising the number of groups into which any activity should logically fit was necessary. Ultimately, it arrived at six headline groups. The groups required testing across a select quantity of organisations representing several sectors to ensure consistency as the process continued.

Finally, having already discovered the three core elements all started with 'P', and being a fan of the *Keep It Simple* philosophy, it became essential to have all nine elements begin with a 'P'. Five of the next six were already apparent, Policies, Practices & Performance, Product & Promotion.

The only outlier was governance, an outworking of Purpose. Fortunately, the core motive for corporate governance is protection. Corporate governance is the set of mechanisms, processes and relations used by various parties to control and operate a corporation. So, I determined that The Model would refer to governance as Protection.

I then focused on the remaining development and testing by:

- Determining and proving the position of each operational element
- The prominent impacting factors of each element to its cohort elements

What is the power of The P9 Management Model?

Simplicity and robustness are its most vital characteristics. Still, it is all about aspirational outcomes of sustainable excellence by substantially improving the daily decisions you and your management team make. It truly is a paradigm change, gradually producing game-changing results.

Imagine if every manager had access to a tool, from middle management upwards, that would equip them with the organisational keys to purpose-driven sustainable excellence. Imagine if your senior management understood every 'P' element and its powerful influence on each other. Imagine being able to measure the performance contribution of each element, and then having identified an under-performing area, being able to consider the impact of a potential solution on an organisational-wide basis before implementing the same.

So, having already introduced to you the loose influence of science in identifying and grouping the nine Ps, let me now explain The Model's connection to the engineering discipline. Equilateral and isosceles triangles are the primary shapes for strength and stability in structural engineering.

As already shown above, The Model's structure is made up of one primary equilateral triangle representing Purpose, People & Processes, each having an apex that interconnects with its own equilateral secondary triangle to illuminate two additional unique operational elements (six in total), which then are all directly linked through their own isosceles triangles.

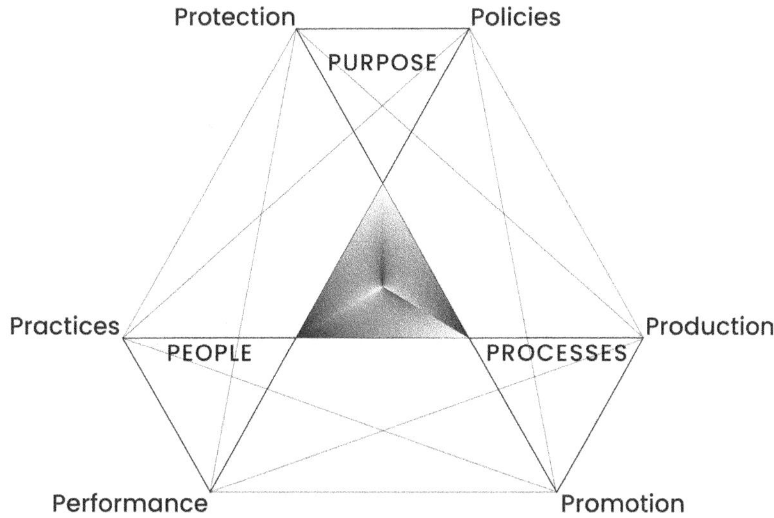

Those isosceles triangles share strength and stability, linking all the operational elements. Together these links demonstrate the reliance upon every other element. This diagrammatic structure was what some peers and clients began referring to as The Diamond View. The Model illustrates that not one of these six elements is wholly superior nor totally independent. The success of each operational element is interdependent on the success of the others.

Each one is a 'heavy lifter'; whose objectives are clear and measurable, whose performance needs to be consistently high, and whose contribution deserves organisational-wide respect, indeed, to be honoured.

Each element has a uniquely impacting relationship with each of the other elements.

When developing each of The Model's descriptive relational impact phrases (all thirty-six), there was a considered and exhaustive process in observations, experiences, reflection, and consultative testing.

In the following chapters, you will have the opportunity to view and consider these thirty-six relationships in detail and then meditate on their current critical influence affecting your organisation's performance.

Both consideration and meditation? Really? Yes, 'consideration' will build (incrementally) your knowledge and capacity to accurately articulate each element's role and importance. Consequently, you will go far beyond just having the ability to quote them. Your investment in 'meditating' on each one, and its impacts, will empower you to apply plans, policies, and practices across your organisation to deliver the desired outcomes.

As stated in my Preface, the reader I seek will already be serious about management and leadership. There are no real-world shortcuts to organisational excellence, and becoming a P9 Management Model Graduate will take more than the time it takes to read this book.

Just as being an operative in the pinnacle league of motor racing, Formula 1, takes considerable investment, commitment, courage, self-confidence, belief and optimism in your equipment and critical team members, so it is with being a follower and enthusiastic user of The P9 Management Model.

However, and fortunately, being an enthusiastic user of The Model is not a burdensome experience. Indeed, once you are across its architecture, along with the relational impacts of all its elements, and become familiar and comfortable with its methods and paradigms, you will find yourself very comfortable in your role as a driver of a finely tuned machine.

The Model's quick reference guide lists the thirty-six headline declarations.

Relational Factors of The P9 Management Model													
CORE		Purpose →	1	***merits*** Protection	2	***drives*** Policies	*A worthy & defined **Purpose** delivered by valued **People** utilising highly developed **Processes** = organisational success leading to sustainable excellence!*						
		People →	3	***perform*** Practices	4	***determine*** Performance							
		Processes →	5	***create*** Production	6	***deploy*** Promotion							
OPERATIONAL	PURPOSE {	Protection →	7	***steers*** Policies	8	***reviews*** Practices	9	***enhances*** Performance	10	***guides*** Production	11	***monitors*** Promotion
		Policies →	12	***reflect*** Protection	13	***influence*** Practices	14	***affect*** Performance	15	***guard*** Production	16	***regulate*** Promotion
	PEOPLE {	Practices →	17	***raise*** Protection	18	***strengthen*** Policies	19	***impact*** Performance	20	***shape*** Production	21	***control*** Promotion
		Performance →	22	***submits to*** Protection	23	***shadows*** Policies	24	***follows*** Practices	25	***supports*** Production	26	***stimulates*** Promotion
	PROCESSES {	Production →	27	***considers*** Protection	28	***weighs*** Policies	29	***is subject to*** Practices	30	***moves*** Performance	31	***causes*** Promotion
		Promotion →	32	***yields to*** Protection	33	***obeys*** Policies	34	***is a child of*** Practices	35	***is dependent on*** Performance	36	***improves*** Production

For the sake of practicality, I insisted that the wordiness of each declaration be minimal. Critically, The Model's quick reference guide has limited strength if you only view it as a theory. It gives you powerfully factual information, but it remains a theory until it becomes applied knowledge gained through the personal experience of regular use.

As outlined above, The Model represents nine umbrella elements (3 primary & 6 operational). It is not the end picture, not the extensive view. As shown in the expanded view example below (second layer), each of the six operational elements has numerous other relational components. Indeed, an expanded third layer of specifics exists. For example, HR Management will likely include Recruitment, Administration, Benefits, Health & Safety, Rewards & Recognition, Training & External Education, and Reporting. Actually, in larger organisations, a fourth layer is often present.

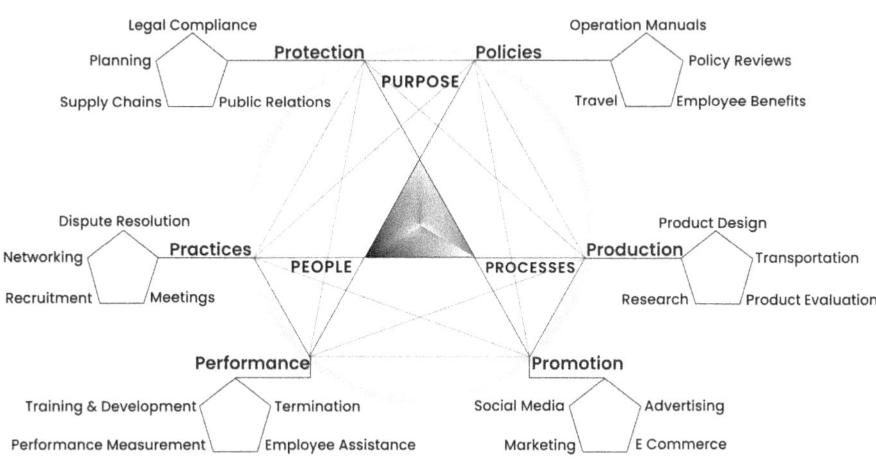

Now is an opportune moment to **again stress that The P9 Management Model is the Think Big view of your organisation. It does not represent specific divisions or departments but critical umbrella areas of management responsibility**. Indeed, it is likely that every division or department will have its engagement with, and utilise, each 'P' element. It is a sophisticated and philosophical approach to management that empowers your quest for knowledge and wisdom, and improves your ability to deal with obstacles.

The Model helps focus senior managers on the known prerequisite organisational umbrellas.

It allows managers to memorise them quickly and thus have them consistently in the forefront of their minds and, more importantly, to have an ever-present desire to ensure every P element succeeds.

Because The Model is the global view approach, it does, when correctly applied, minimise the negative impact of the age-old issue of competing silos within an organisation because your Executive Management Team and your divisional/departmental managers have a significantly deeper appreciation of how the performance of each and every other division/department, has a direct impact on their division's/department's ability to perform. Further entrenching this experience, The Model encourages joint responsibility, primarily by your senior management team, then filtering down to middle management or team leaders (depending on your organisational structure). However, blatantly, the overriding responsibility stops at the CEO's desk for The Model's end effectiveness and its impact on the organisation's performance.

Consequently, it motivates each manager to do whatever is in their ability to contribute to the success of every other area. More on this topic in a later chapter titled The P9 Cohesive Management Culture.

By the way, The P9 Cohesive Management Culture is a crucial part of The Model, incorporating inter-department *Consideration, Communication, Cooperation, Contribution, & Celebration* (the subjects of the later chapter).

Once managers fully understand and enthusiastically embrace The Model with a strong desire to achieve its rewarding outcomes, they:

- Continue to take ownership of the responsibility to optimise their division's/department's share of contribution to the organisation's results
- Quickly and tangibly adopting **The P9 Cohesive Management Culture** mentality, they seek opportunities to assist managers of other areas

R.Q. *Are you able to quickly identify areas of underperformance in your organisation?* ***W.I.D.***

R.Q. *What are they, and how do you presently manage them?* ***W.I.D.***

As a brief introduction, this P9 Cohesive Management Culture mindset produces 'issue' consideration, inter-department transparent communication, active cooperation, high-level contribution and expressive celebration. It is a top-down culture led by the senior manager, who regularly demonstrates their firm commitment to assist all the other departments in excelling. Highly successful organisations can be the result of understanding and managing these 9Ps exceptionally well. This objective is one reason for regularly repeating the 9Ps in their full wording throughout this book so that readers can recall and speak to each element without hesitation.

So far, I have only focused on the strength of The P9 Management Model, the understanding and valuing of each P element's critically important position and the relational factors. I have only referred to the triangular structural aspects of The Model because until these become identified and accepted, linking all the elements by way of an outer circle remains unseen.

Sideline*: I am a road cyclist, admittedly not the fastest. I am often associated with a demographic group nicknamed Mamil (middle-aged man in lycra), or in my case, even perhaps more sadly as a Samil (Senior aged man in lycra).*

I sincerely appreciate my bicycle wheels' required strength and perfect balance. Specifically, my bike's rear wheel, the driving wheel through which power gets to the road surface. I can easily see my front wheel (the bike's steering wheel) when riding my bike. It is more difficult to see the rear wheel easily. Yet, it is through the rear wheel that my energised power contacts the road surface, thus producing the desired product that the bicycle makes: forward motion.

A current mid-spec carbon fibre framed bike with lightweight wheels has an all-up weight of only seven kilograms. The components of the wheel are the central hub, the spokes, and the tyre-wrapped rim. Any structural imperfections cause the wheel to become buckled. When travelling downhill on a bitumen road at 60-70 KPH on a seven-kilogram bike, you want perfectly round wheels between you and that road. If you are going uphill, you want every ounce of your hard-working energy delivered efficiently to the road surface. A flat-spotted tyre or a buckled wheel can dramatically inhibit the power delivery; the result is poor performance and increased fatigue.

Suppose you think of The Model's parts as components of a wheel. In that case, the three core elements of Purpose, People and Processes form the central hub. Their relational connections to the operational P's are the spokes, and the operational Ps connect to the rim.

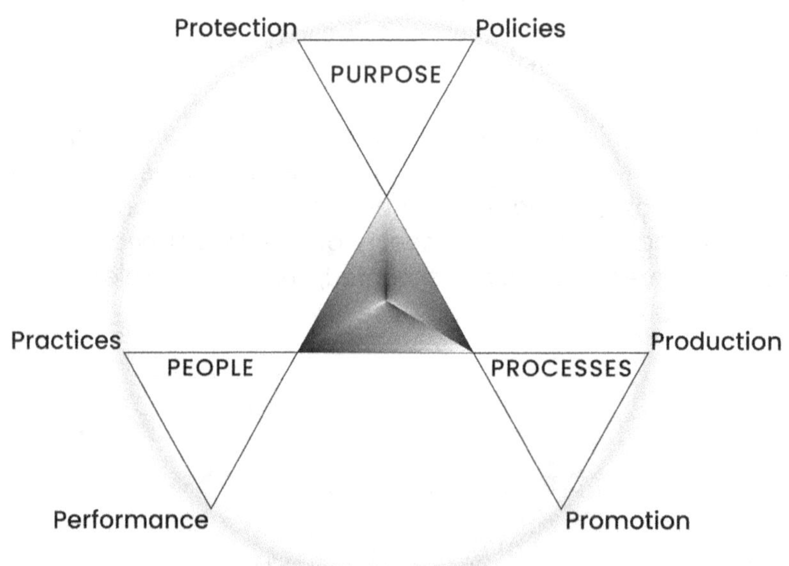

That brings us to the perfect P9 Management Model outcomes, which enables all the triangulated elements to fit within a finely tuned wheel flawlessly, propelling an organisation forward at an enviable pace.

The P9 rim is the final brush touch, the light bulb moment. It highlights how the ideally located and interdependently related operational elements form the rounded organisation's wheel of excellence, enabling it to withstand obstacles and accelerate it forward. Indeed, you have a perfect wheel only when you remove the flat spots of misalignment.

When tuning a spoked wheel, to make it truly round, you adjust the length and tension of each spoke until they deliver a perfectly round and aligned wheel. The same logic applies to The P9 Management Model. The spokes extend from the hub (the three primary elements) to the virtual rim (wrapped around the six operational elements).

To achieve Organisational Excellence, you must ensure that these six operational elements, Protection, Policies, Product, Promotion, Performance and Practices, are correctly aligned, equally valued, and all achieve their objective purpose.

This measure of Organisational Excellence is assessed by systematically analysing their performance and relative contribution using values of 1 through to 9, where 1 represents 'poor performance' and 9 means' outstanding performance'. Each element has different factors requiring assessment, which can vary between organisations.

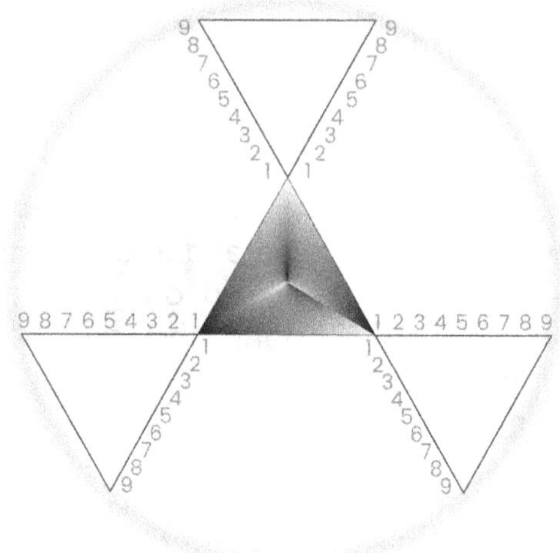

Imagine the buckled outcome of the wheel if every element had different values. Again, I believe this is precisely how most organisations operate.

Let us consider an example of an established and profitable company building project homes.

Hypothetically, the company enjoys a reputation for delivering well-designed and constructed houses (Product = 9). Their marketing is reasonably practical and extensive (Promotion = 8). They have highly valued, experienced staff who achieve consistently good outputs (Performance = 8) and are well aware of workplace safety and maintaining a desirable culture (Practices = 7). However, while they desire and believe in good governance (Protection = 7), they have underdeveloped and inconsistent policies (Policies = 6). Applying those values to The Model would result in an out-of-round wheel, which causes confusion, forgetfulness, indifference, indecision, non-compliance, under-performance and costly mistakes.

It only takes one undervalued or underperforming P element to buckle the wheel. History shows many companies with excellent products ended their journey in insolvency because management neglected one or more of their 9Ps. However, most organisations survive without ever achieving a genuinely rounded performance wheel. They remain average, just as you can still ride a bike with a slightly buckled wheel.

So, to sum up, the answer to the question; ***What is the power of The P9 Management Model?*** The power factors are numerous, including:

1. You will gain a thorough understanding and value of each P element
2. The ability to refer to, or quickly recall, the relational impacts
3. Your management can create the ideal and accurate alignment of every P element
4. You have the ability, accompanied by a matrix tool, for you and your management team to become exceptionally good and consistent decision-makers
5. You develop a cohesive and enviable workplace culture
6. For you, the CEO, to be a leader of qualities leading quality leaders, thus assuring a high-performing organisation of excellence

The following nine chapters consider each P element and its detailed relational importance.

2
PURPOSE MANAGEMENT

> *"He who has a why to live for can bear almost any how."*
> **Friedrich Nietzsche**, German philosopher

> **Critical Note:** Please do not expect to find your organisation's purpose in this chapter. Defining the purpose of your organisation is too uniquely exclusive to obtain in a book.

R.Q. *What automatically comes to your mind when you think of the purpose of your organisation?* ***W.I.D.***

R.Q. *Presently, would you say your organisation's purpose permeates all parts of your organisation?* ***W.I.D.***

R.Q. *If I asked a recently employed team member to explain your organisation's purpose, what would you expect as a typical response?* ***W.I.D.***

Introduction

Before getting too far into this topic, I must explain what I mean when referring to an organisation's purpose. A commonly accepted definition of purpose is *"the reason for which something is done or created or for which something exists"*. I have learnt that purpose can be an excellent guide to making personal life-changing decisions. Purpose can influence your behaviour while also influencing the behaviour of others. Purpose can also shape your goals by offering a clean and clear sense of direction. At an organisational level, those same attributes of Purpose apply. Purpose incorporates ideals of betterment and delivers meaning that often inspires the collective committed to such standards to persist and push through otherwise impenetrable obstacles.

My experience makes me confident to state that Purpose defines an organisation. An organisation that does not begin with a specific, well-defined, developed, and meaningful purpose rarely reaches a desirable outcome, that alone, sustainable excellence. Indeed, that revelation of understanding the importance of Purpose motivated me to invest years of observation, research, and assessment of organisational purpose. It was also a significant factor that enabled me to develop a management model that would deliver outstanding outcomes by prioritising the pinnacle positioning and value of organisational purpose.

Alignment

The Model illustrates the equilateral secondary triangle from **Purpose,** integrating with **Protection** (Governance) and **Policies**. Another way of putting it is that Protection and Policies are Purpose's out-workings. Purpose *merits* Protection and Purpose *drives* Policies.

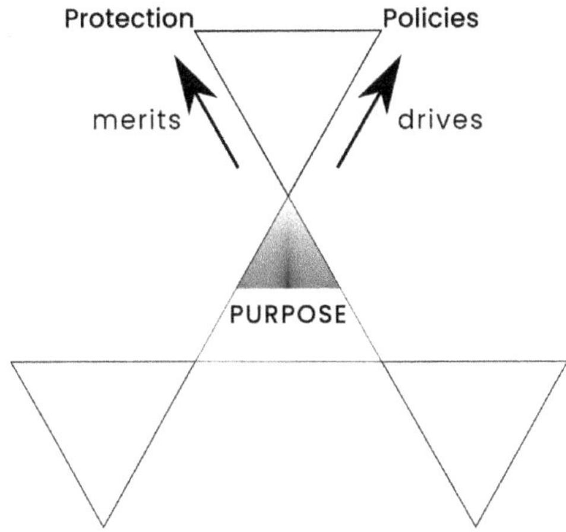

The remaining four operational elements of The Model, Practices, Performance, Product, and Promotion, are directly linked to your organisation's purpose through its elements of Protection and Policies.

As often as the opportunity arises, I promote the idea of crafting an organisation's 'why' factor in a Purpose Statement, a statement that effectively communicates why your organisation exists, what drives it to continual improvement and a striving for excellence.

Vision and Mission statements received substantial attention from senior managers, consultants and academics in the final decades of the last millennium. Most organisations that invested time thoughtfully developing their Vision and Mission Statements and then committing to those statements and aligning them to their values benefited from the results.

Following are questions that arise when developing a Vision Statement (*questions provided by company profiling and funding entity, FundingSage* [5])

- *What problem does my organisation seek to solve?*
- *Why do I believe this problem needs to address?*

---

5 FundingSage - https://fundingsage.com/clarify-the-vision-10-questions-to-create-an-effective-vision-statement/

- *Does this problem matter to other people?*
- *Do I honestly believe we have the answer to that problem?*
- *Are there changes I believe my organisation can make?*
- *What are the greatest strengths of my organisation?*
- *What is my dream for this organisation?*
- *How would things be different if my dream came true?*
- *Does my dream connect on a personal level with others?*

By reading the above, you can see that these questions are granular and personalised. They are primarily practical and result orientated.

In contrast, the philosophy of a Purpose Statement is considerably more foundational and far-reaching in its intent. If you have not yet developed and articulated a purpose for your organisation, here are just a few questions that should assist you:

- *Why was this organisation/division/department created?*
- *What solution does it deliver?*
- *Who directly and indirectly benefits from this organisation's/ division's/department's activities?*
- *How does it beneficially change your communities?*
- *What size hole would be left in the communities you engage with if your organisation ceased to exist?*
- *What price is the organisation willing to pay to hold steadfast to its purpose?*

Purpose-driven organisations, committed to a pathway of continual improvement and a goal of sustainable excellence, promptly provide accurately qualified and demonstrated answers to these and similarly strategic questions.

There is also a trend for organisations to write a core values statement, which many management consultants (I concur with) promote as a best practice approach. There is a fifth Organisational Statement that I recommend CEOs develop, the Workplace Culture Statement, covered in the People Management chapter later. However, in my opinion, far too few operatives currently prosecute the case for a Purpose Statement.

Each statement must have a principle objective. Following is my helpful, quick reference guide for constructing organisational statements.

Organisational Statements					
Focus	**Purpose**	**Vision**	**Mission**	**Core Values**	**Workplace Culture**
Aim	why we exist	what we intend to be	how we will do it	what we are	how we live it
Timeline	all	future: medium & long term	present, medium-term	all	all
Task	declaration	inspiration	education	dedication	application

Some typical questions arise:

- *Which statement/s should my organisation have?*
- *Do we need all five?*
- *Should we combine some or all into one statement?*

Unfortunately, I cannot answer these questions without:

- Fully exploring the thinking of the creator of your organisation (if possible) or, in their absence, the Board's chairperson and current CEO
- Studying your organisation's idiosyncrasies to assist you in funnelling your determinations

I can tell you that there are many opinions about whether you need a Vision Statement and Mission Statement, a combined Vision Statement and Mission Statement, or neither.

Purpose

This chapter intends to assist you in understanding the value of having a real purpose and creating a greater appreciation for the immeasurable need for managing Purpose well.

To start with another 'P' would be sacrilegious to organisational success! My primary business mantra is this; **an Organisation = Purpose** plus **People** plus **Processes**. It is both a formula, and it is my philosophy. The prioritised position of Purpose is wholly intentional because Purpose is the foundational cornerstone upon which all the other elements are constructed.

When it comes to organisations, **if the first element of Purpose is absent, you do not need the following two**; in the absence of purpose, you do not need people or processes because if an organisation does not have a purpose, it should not exist. It will indeed not become a highly successful organisation of excellence. You might judge my opinion on this matter as harsh, but it results from decades of observation. Yes, most organisations have a purpose, but if it is not driving the organisation, the purpose is weak, misguided, or the organisation has lost its way.

Again, purpose is the reason for which something is done or created. Whether it applies to individuals or organisations, purpose provides a sense of determination. Purpose should be the nucleus of an organisation, the foundational cornerstone upon which an organisation exists. Purpose drives an organisation; it can unite and inspire you and your team to excel. Purpose outlives individuals, be they the creator, current chair of the Board, current CEO, or any other senior role. Purpose permeated throughout an organisation can overcome negativity and doubt. It will navigate people to the predetermined performance waypoints.

If you accept all that, then the logical questions that follow should be:

- What are the components of purpose?
- How do the relational components of purpose influence? That is, what does and how does purpose impact?
- How do I manage purpose?

- How do I sell (communicate, promote) purpose?
- If necessary, how do I change the purpose?

This chapter addresses the points listed in the above questions, ensuring adequate attention to detail. I have learnt that presuming someone understands purpose just by discussing it at a concept level is a big mistake. Purpose deserves whatever investment of study and deliberation time it takes for you to appreciate all its parts, position, and power.

Components of Organisational Purpose requiring management

If you can imagine purpose as a massive table with several legs, you will recognise that each leg has a part to play and adds overall stability and strength to the table. I can identify seven distinct components that, in my opinion, codify organisational purpose, and they are:

1. **Ownership**

   Ownership of the purpose of an organisation will depend on the sector.

   Clearly, in the public sector at State and Federal levels, the ownership of why a government department is needed will be a product of political, constitutional or legislative factors. State and Federal government agencies are similar, while Local Governments are again a product of legislation.

   However, for purpose to have real value, it needs a human face, a person full of passion and dedication. At State and Federal levels, while the Ministers of departments are responsible for facing the television cameras and articulating a particular position, response or defence, there has long been tension between the politicians and departmental directors caused by differing motivations or agendas. Although politicians of a particular persuasion appoint departmental directors, those directors often outlive their masters and serve under the next minister (regularly of a different persuasion) and then occasionally the next minister. Ultimately, I believe it is essentially the departmental director who must have ownership of the purpose for which their department exists. They must drive the culture and performance of their department. This approach applies equally to State and Federal government agencies.

Local Government authorities are technically like their State and Federal counterparts. Their CEOs (sometimes still called General Managers) are appointed either by their elected Councillors (politicians) or by a popular vote of their community (ratepayers), depending on their jurisdiction. Although in my experience, due to the community nature of Local Governments, Mayors can have more significant influence and direct the impact on the purpose-driven culture of their organisation. So, in local government, I have learnt that the ownership of the purpose is more often subject to the peculiarities and dynamics of the organisation.

In NFP (not-for-profit) organisations, the ownership of the purpose for forming the entity can vary greatly. For instance, with some charities, the purpose of the charity will have been determined by their parent institution. The purpose of most highly reputable charities came out of a response to a humanitarian or environmental crisis. So it was up to the creating founders to determine and articulate such a purpose. However, suppose the founders are no longer present at an operational level. In that case, the board's role remains to take ownership of their organisation's purpose, coexisting with the current CEO adopting a solid sense of ownership.

Finally, in the for-profit sector, a larger organisation's purpose needs ownership by both the CEO and the Chair of the Board; depending on the size or history of the organisation, this can be the same person.

Other individuals in the organisation may share a sense of ownership of its purpose. In highly successful organisations, you will observe that most staff truly understand their organisation's purpose; they buy in and agree with it. They also own it.

With ownership comes responsibility. If you believe in the purpose of your organisation, you will do whatever you can to progress it. You will promote it at every opportunity; you'll champion its cause. You will speak on its benefit and why you believe it is beneficial for others. You will fight for its longevity and protect its reputation.

Ownership of Purpose will deliver an attractional and infectious sense of pride.

2. **Intentionality**

Purpose must be intentional to have any real value. So, what is the intention of your organisation? What is the fundamental reason your organisation exists? Who or what does your organisation benefit? What is the primary and secondary intention if your organisation exists for more than one purpose? Intentionality counts!

Your purpose must be the product of mentally determining the desired result. Therefore, the purpose needs to be specific regarding its intent.

Your purpose needs to be intentionally clear and precise. If your organisation's purpose is not clear in your mind, it will never be apparent in the minds of others. Clarity of purpose often needs a considerable investment of time and focus. It usually needs to be carefully considered and developed. And then it needs to be redeveloped, and then redeveloped again. It is a honing exercise. Like any precision tool, it takes many skills to build it. An idea cannot be a purpose until it is clear and precise. This task takes intentionality.

Your purpose needs to be intentionally communicable. Your purpose needs to be deliberately transferable. I deal with these aspects in the following sub-headings.

Hopefully, you are beginning to get the point. Be intentional when developing your organisation's purpose; be very deliberate.

3. **Centrality**

The purpose of your organisation should be at the centre of every aspect of every area of every section of your organisation. Purpose is the DNA of your organisation. Purpose needs to permeate every person, every part, every policy, every practice, and every product of your organisation.

Purpose should be the mirror image that all plans, processes and practices replicate. When I am offered guided tours of an organisation's operation and introduced to various team members, as often as possible, I will ask them this question; how does what you do reconcile to the organisation's purpose? The next moments shout volumes about the organisation.

In highly successful organisations, the response is clear and relevant, indicating that the organisation's purpose is discussed regularly. Further, it is a crucial value in explaining the activity to me.

The answers or lack thereof in less successful organisations paint a different story. The responses or lack thereof indicate that the organisation's purpose is either unknown or not fully understood, not considered daily, and not valued as essential to the current task.

How central is your organisation's purpose? If I wandered the workspaces of your organisation randomly interviewing your people about the relationship of the organisation's purpose to what they are currently doing, what answers would I hear?

4. **Simplicity**

Your organisation's purpose must be simple, straightforward and easily understood by your team. Perhaps more than in any other matter, it is essential that your purpose at its core be simple for it to be accepted and valued. So much has been written about the benefits of the KIS principle. You do not have to be a qualified psychologist to understand that this is true. You experience it daily. Keeping things as simple as possible creates efficiencies and reliabilities, two desirable purpose qualities.

You do not want only your Executive Management Team to understand and comply with the purpose of your organisation; you want every team member to be fully on-board and apply it at every opportunity.

Simplicity delivers repetition, precisely what you need. You want the consideration of your organisation's purpose to be perpetually present throughout all activities undertaken daily, monthly, quarterly, and annually. Repeat it until everyone knows it is the DNA of your organisation.

R.Q. *If I were to conduct an organisation-wide survey on the simplicity of your organisation's purpose, rating it with a score of 1 to 9 (1 being hard to understand and 9 being very easy to understand), what would you expect findings to be? Does this concern you? Would it concern your key stakeholders?* ***W.I.D.***

R.Q. *How would you rate your organisation's purpose? Does your organisation's purpose need to be simplified? What can you do to improve the facilitation of your organisation's purpose?* ***W.I.D.***

Simplification is worth striving for when it comes to your organisation's purpose!

5. **Worth**

This topic is all about the value of your organisation's purpose.

You will have read or heard about intrinsic and extrinsic value; you may have even studied what they mean. It is the essence of a philosophical branch known as Axiology. *"Axiology is the study of value, or goodness, in its widest sense. The distinction is commonly made between intrinsic and extrinsic value - i.e., between that which is valuable for its own sake, and that which is valuable only as a means to something else, which itself may be extrinsically or intrinsically valuable"* (source unknown).

This understanding is a critical point for the manager serious about organisational performance. *Is my organisation's purpose valuable for its own sake? Does it really have standalone value? Or, by necessity, is it a means to something else? Is one right and the other wrong?* I suggest that the critical point here is to have your organisation's purpose be of enviable value.

High-performance organisations have purposes considered of high value and great worth. A purpose that benefits many people is significantly more worthy than a purpose that helps a single person or just a few individuals. A common but questionable purpose is "my organisation's purpose is to make me wealthy". While wealth may be a primary motive for the creators of a for-profit organisation, should it become its purpose? *If so, would you consider it of intrinsic or extrinsic value?* Your answer matters.

If an organisation's purpose is the mirror image that all plans, processes and practices replicate, then the value you place on it will permeate the entire organisation. This mindset is equally appropriate if you consider it of little or great value. If you do not value your organisation's purpose highly, your team will certainly not value it. Likewise, if you place and demonstrate that you highly value your organisation's purpose, it is reasonable to believe that your team will also put a high value on it.

6. **Communicable** (I know it is not a proper English language word, but it works)

This aspect is the frontline of purpose; is your organisation's purpose communicable? It aligns with the simplicity component explained in point 4 above; is your organisation's purpose simple enough to communicate? If your answer is not an immediate "yes", I suggest you most assuredly have an organisational purpose problem.

Most organisations will either have a Vision Statement, a Mission Statement, or both. There is considerable marketplace content about both topics; you will not have to look hard to find an expert guest speaker on either issue. Recently I put visionary leadership in the search engine on Amazon.com's website, resulting in a list of 4,929 books related to the subject; seriously, try it.

But which comes first, vision or purpose? It is not an unreasonable question. Is one the product of the other? Does one drive the other? Is there truly a Genesis order between the two? As an intentional manager, is it essential for you to hold a view on this matter? I believe it is, and this is an appropriate time to share my opinion on the subject. I consider that purpose comes first.

Purpose creates the vision of an organisation. Vision is the vehicular currency of purpose. It carries the purpose and trades on the purpose. Vision, when communicated effectively, articulates the purpose. When we talk about

Organisational Performance, purpose overrides everything else. Purpose is core. Purpose is paramount.

Purpose communicated through an articulated vision is often the difference between capable small businesses and flourishing larger organisations. So, it starts with the CEO, or Divisional/Departmental Director, developing methods of communicating the organisation's purpose by painting word pictures that all recipients easily imagine.

Purpose Statements that can move organisations forward have common attributes being:

- Beyond the organisation itself, benefits that impact
- Imagery that motivates team members to outperform previous results continually
- Imagery that moves customers/clients to want to do business
- Imagery that inspires and directs change

Whatever the price, developing a sustainable Purpose Statement is worth it. Once determined, developing vision communication techniques becomes a priority and an exercise worthy of time and resource investment.

Interweaving purpose-related vision into all aspects of your organisation is a critical key that requires intent, attention, and commitment. Having a great purpose but not having all your stakeholders know about it is comparable to having no vision, no purpose.

7. **Transferable**

You might consider I dealt with this component in point 1 above, Ownership, and you would be correct in part. However, there is more to having your organisation's purpose transferrable than point 1 majored in. The latter part of the Ownership section focused on staff taking possession of the purpose, which is an admirable objective for any organisation.

However, to go beyond that, I regularly advise on developing an organisational purpose that all stakeholders can understand, relate to, agree with, and take hold of. This approach should be the ultimate goal of organisational purpose, well beyond primary performance targets. This methodology is the sphere of exceptional thinking, where intentional managers think of organisational success as more significant, more impacting, and greater benefit than profit or performance alone.

Your organisation's purpose needs to be inspirational. You need a purpose that exudes authenticity, credibility, intentionality, greatness, and value, suggesting inclusion, not exclusion, altruism, not greed. Let us not become delusional here; this is not an easy achievement. It is worth aiming for, nevertheless.

The key is understanding that purpose has two core qualities: principle and practice. The previous paragraph refers to the principle of purpose. However, the transferability of purpose relies upon its practice. How is it rolled out? It must adequately address the other six components:

- Ownership
- Intentionality
- Centrality
- Simplicity
- Worth
- Communicability

Is there a purpose culture within your organisation? Is your organisation's purpose a regular coffee stop conversation? Do your senior management regularly review awareness of purpose within your organisation? How aware of your organisation's purpose are your clients? How aware of your organisation's purpose are your distribution channel partners? How aware of your organisation's purpose is your advertising agency? Your lawyers, bankers, auditors?

> Is your organisation's purpose transparently apparent in all your policies and procedures? Does your promotional material reflect your organisation's purpose? What processes do you/will you have to address the preceding questions?

There you have it; seven critical components of purpose that have a lineal impact on your organisation's success. You may consider that there are additional components that I have not identified. If so, and you can substantiate them, I gladly accept that. Those seven components combined above are the ones that I have observed made a positive difference in several highly successful organisations. I am also an avid reader of business case studies that confirm that an organisation's purpose directly affects its performance capabilities and outcomes.

If you can determine your organisation's purpose, I would say congratulations because it is a huge privilege that only a few experience. Then, I recommend you use each described component above as a filter or checklist to ensure that you provide every opportunity for your organisation to excel.

For the rest of you, let me encourage you to seriously consider this chapter's contents and determine whether there are items raised that will assist you in managing purpose in a new or enhanced fashion, enabling more success within your organisation.

Relational Components of Organisational Purpose

Is it essential to understand the relationship between each 'P'? I say, of course, it is. Is it worth analysing the impact of each 'P'? Yes, it is! This discipline is management at its core, understanding and manipulating critical influence factors within your control, affecting your organisation within and beyond. Purpose is at the top of the list. It is foundational and fundamentally critical to your organisation's existence; it is your lifeline. Lose it or get it radically wrong, and your organisation will flat line.

At its core foundational level, you now know that my position is that an Organisation = Purpose plus People plus Processes. So I believe (and will prove) that there is a direct relationship between

Purpose, People, and Processes; a relationship of such importance as to underpin the performance outcomes and overall success of your organisation's people and processes. Let me begin this section by focusing on the relationships between Purpose and People and between Purpose and Processes.

The seven components of purpose detailed above provide the idiosyncrasies of purpose. In a way, they describe the cause and character of purpose. Beyond just getting to know it, they help you become more intimate with organisational purpose. Organisational purpose should be your close friend, although I have known or known of CEOs who have felt so constrained by their organisation's purpose to blame it for less than satisfactory performance results. Nevertheless, organisational purpose is the inseparable companion of senior management.

Those same seven components combined might persuasively sustain the argument that purpose stands alone in its identifiable right; purpose is wholly independent. I can think of at least one compelling reason for believing in the independence of purpose. If you have ever personally or even been part of a team that has created a new organisation, you will appreciate the effort invested in deciding that entity's name. An organisation's name has great value. It is its identity deemed to be directly related to the success of an organisation.

However, if you have had experience changing the name (rebranding) of a successfully established large organisation, you will know the invested effort. You would probably have instructed a globally recognised leader in public relations such as Edelman or Ogilvy to undertake considerable discreet research and survey work to develop recommendations. Such professionals would begin by determinedly investigating the purpose of your organisation. You do not lightly change an established organisation's name; it should never be a whimsical matter. It requires a strategic, structured, and disciplined approach. I know this because I have managed these critical organisational changes and advised senior management on rebranding.

While challenging, there is a growing number of organisations that have successfully changed their names, including the following:

- Google: The world's #1 search engine was created in 1996 under the name "BackRub" it was renamed "Google" in 1999
- IBM: Computing Tabulating Recording Corporation was renamed "International Business Machines" (IBM) in 1924
- Pepsi: In 1898, Brad's Drink was renamed "Pepsi-Cola"
- Telstra: In 1993, Australia's monopoly telecommunications carrier (Telecom) changed its international operations name to "Telstra" and in 1995 repeated it in its home nation

My point is this; purpose outlives everything within an organisation, including its name. I would even go so far as to prosecute the case that within an organisation, purpose should be the main masthead, the flag of principle that flies higher than any other, yes, even higher than your organisation's name.

Naturally, I hope you understand the idiosyncrasies and the often perceived independence of organisational purpose. Yet, we need now to consider the interdependency of organisational purpose.

In the first component of purpose (ownership), I proposed that "for purpose to have real value, it needs a human face". Hence purpose is reliant upon people. The first relational component of Purpose is People. People carry purpose. People perform out of purpose. People will give sacrificially for purpose. People have died for purpose. But for purpose to profoundly impact people, it needs to have perceived value, another stated component (worth) of purpose.

R.Q. *Would you agree that the regular contact between People and organisational purpose will be critically important to achieving the objectives of the purpose? Why?* ***W.I.D.***

This precept depends upon the intentionality, centrality, simplicity, worth, communicability and transferability components of purpose. Unless all these (people) components of purpose are regularly present, would you agree that you are undercooking your organisation's potential?

Now let us consider the relationship between Purpose and the Processes undertaken within your organisation. A process can be a task, a method or repeated actions; anything an organisation performs which doesn't logically or efficiently sit under the Purpose or People categories.

So, think of a process within your organisation. Any process! Then consider its relationship to your organisation's purpose. I'll give you an example; dealing with a complainant on an incoming telephone call; they could be a client, customer, supply or distribution chain operative, or perhaps a community member perceivably burdened by your organisation. These relatively low fruit tasks are significantly impacted by the centrality component of your organisation's purpose; 'Purpose should be the mirror image which all plans, processes and practices replicate'. Suppose your organisation's purpose is present in the mind of your team member handling the call. In that case, the approach will comply with the purpose and likely progress the matter in a mutually beneficial manner.

You might consider the above example too basic or simplistic; perhaps you think it is just management 101. I would disagree. Highly successful organisations excel in the macro-management areas of strategy and economics and the finest detail of the most straightforward task. Such excellence is driven by purpose!

Therefore, I submit that Purpose and Processes are linked wholeheartedly.

I could (and will do in later chapters) equally advance the substantial argument for the relationship between Purpose and each of the remaining components of Protection, Policies, Practices, Performance, Product, and Promotion. Hopefully, I have already transcribed sufficiently to prove my view. The concluding point here is to challenge you to assess the presence and effectiveness of your organisation's relational components of Purpose.

Selling Purpose

There is a book in this one sub-heading because, according to Amazon.com's website, a list of 4,929 books exist on visionary leadership. To what I imagine is your delight, I will aim to be concise while covering the essentials. I like to break this area up into two underlying methods of selling purpose; tangible and intangible, or if you prefer, direct and indirect.

I refer to tangibly selling purpose as someone's verbal action or other direct means of communication; printed on paper, cards, posters, banners, billboards, electronically illuminated on monitors (small, large, and huge), smartphones and tablets. It will be the spoken word used in casual conversation, informal and formal meetings, interviews, speeches, debates, promotions, advertising, training, sales and general negotiations, human resource reviews, reviews of processes, Etc. Are you across this? At every opportunity in every situation by every conceivable team member, give attention to the possibility of selling purpose. Sorry, more concisely, **never stop selling your organisation's purpose**. Print it as a separate Purpose Statement or partially in the organisation's vision or mission statements, strategic master plans, operational plans, policies, procedure manuals, training manuals, technical manuals, administrative documentation, promotional material, meeting agendas, etc. Are you totally across this? **Never, never ever, never ever ever stop selling your organisation's purpose.** That is what I mean when I refer to tangibly selling purpose.

Alternately and coexisting is the intangible selling of purpose. I mean anything that promotes or advances the organisation's purpose other than the spoken or written word; anything by any means.

Examples of the intangible selling of purpose include your organisation's working atmosphere, which I argue is part of, but not the totality of an organisation's culture.

After that, the general culture of your organisation includes:

- The unspoken and unwritten practices of your organisation
- The unscripted automatic reactions to unexpected and unwelcomed obstacles to progress by every individual on your team
- The universal level of optimism and 'can-do' attitudes that permeate your organisation
- The aims and intentionality of relationships with all external stakeholders
- The determined strategic approach to an enviable reputation development and retention

This intangible selling of purpose is a critical difference between good entities and organisations of excellence.

It starts at the top; it begins with the CEO. Selling organisational purpose must start at the top for the reasons explained above. It depends upon the essential seven components of purpose; ownership, intentionality, centrality, simplicity, worth, communicability and transferability.

Concerning the seven components of organisational purpose, I suggest that the CEO:

1. Must have a universally noticed, transparently obvious ownership of the organisation's purpose to have apparent and earned respect. In addition to their authoritative leverage, they will need to develop and maintain the above-described real-time purpose culture.

2. They must be intentional about every aspect of their organisation's purpose in perception and reality. This form of intentionality is both taught and caught. The CEO will instruct their immediate leadership team on the type, style, and communication methods of their determination, to achieve the objectives of their organisation's purpose.
3. Should be at the sharp edge of ensuring their leadership team includes the organisation's purpose regularly in planning, reviewing, administering, and managing their respective areas. It's a top-down thing, a model intentionally repeated throughout each responsibility level to underpin its centrality.
4. Should ensure regular measurements of the purpose's simplicity in strategically considered areas of the organisation are undertaken to ensure effective operational penetration, universal understanding and expected application of their organisation's purpose.
5. Must highly value their organisation's purpose and demonstrate this in words and actions. Firstly, there can never be a perception of hypocrisy and secondly, to model such consideration of worth to every individual within their organisation and all external stakeholders. In the absence of the CEO valuing their organisation's purpose, it is impossible to believe that other stakeholders will.
6. Must have the capacity and competency to communicate their organisation's purpose effectively to all relevant stakeholders and the community. If they cannot achieve this, it isn't easy to see how the rest of their organisation's members will enthusiastically share their purpose with other colleagues and external stakeholders.
7. Must have the capacity and competency to transfer (regularly) the organisation's purpose to other individuals. As stated in the Components of Purpose section above, the transferability of purpose relies upon its practice. The CEO's responsibility is to determine that it is rolled out and adequately address the other six components: ownership, intentionality, centrality, simplicity, worth, and

communicability. It is the key to achieving organisational-wide saturation of the purpose.

I said that selling purpose starts with the CEO, but it certainly does not finish there. Each of the described components enables, indeed even empowers, the successful adoption of the organisation's purpose by all necessary stakeholders. The objectives of the organisation's purpose will succeed when you persuade staff to persuade. The more people that buy in, the greater the achievements.

Therefore, selling purpose must be the highest priority by all the key influences within an organisation. Sell it or lose it; one of these two options will eventuate.

Managing Purpose

So far in this chapter, I have focused on you becoming informed as to:

- Understanding what Organisational purpose is by providing its components in a detailed and demonstrated manner
- Considering what the relational components of Organisational purpose are, their relative impacts
- The why, where, and how of selling Organisational purpose

For a chapter titled 'Purpose Management', you would be entitled to think that I may have mentioned the concept of managing purpose before now. Why would an author describing himself as an organisational performance advisor make managing purpose the penultimate topic in a chapter titled 'Purpose Management'? Was it unintentional? Be assured few, if any, things I do are consciously unintended. The reason is my view of managing organisational purpose. I believe that managing it becomes rather systematic once you know:

- What your organisation's purpose is, particularly its relational components and impacts
- Why, Where, and How to Sell organisational purpose, internally and externally

Yet, comprehensively effective management of organisational purpose will be possible in and through the systems you develop. But before I describe specific examples of how to manage it, let us consider why managing organisational purpose is necessary.

There are exciting dynamics incorporated into organisational purpose. Time influences its clarity and, ultimately, its definition. Differing agendas can alter its intent. Competing forces can hijack its momentum. Overlooking it can cause it to lose its prominence. Forgetting it can have devastating results. So, managing organisational purpose is not only necessary but also essential.

How might you manage organisational purpose?

Flowcharting organisational purpose will help you highlight where systems will be most effective. Scheduling organisational-wide, purpose-related, and anonymous surveys will identify gaps, misunderstandings and diminishing importance issues. Such surveys need to be targeted at differing duties and responsibilities.

Receiving regular reports on purpose-related matters from departmental or section heads will assist the CEO in monitoring current impacts and prioritisation and ensure that all levels of management are continually purpose-focused.

Occasionally introducing singular purpose topics into daily briefings or morning hub sessions will retain consistency.

An annual organisational Purpose Audit will achieve at least two benefits. Firstly, it will identify any related deficiencies and secondly, it will amplify to everyone the CEO's commitment to having organisational purpose as an ongoing organisation-wide priority.

Surveying external stakeholders will likewise identify deficiencies or underperformance of your objectives.

Having procedural checklists in place in as many locations or events as possible will assist in the quality of message assurance.

You now have six examples of how you might manage your organisational purpose. Depending on the size or type of organisation, I recommend numerous other effective measurement methods for message distribution success.

R.Q. *So, rating it with a score of 1 to 9 (1 being poorly and 9 being highly effective), what value would you give the management of your organisational purpose? Does this concern you?* ***W.I.D.***

R.Q. *If so, what will you do today to change this?* ***W.I.D.***

For some, if not most senior management, this topic of Purpose, this degree of consideration, requires a radical change of their mindset and practices. To become a successful purpose-driven organisation, the recommendations made in this book need to be executed in a way that feels natural, right, and real.

Speaking of change, this brings us to the last topic in this chapter of Purpose Management.

Changing Purpose

As a CEO, even if you only applied my six examples (provided above) of how you might manage organisational purpose, you would be across the crucial matter of knowing; what is the current health of your organisation's purpose? If things were amiss, then you would know. And you are now better equipped to address such an event.

However, sometimes you need to change your organisation's purpose incrementally. More rarely is the need to change your organisation's purpose radically. Either way, everything this chapter provides will allow you to appreciate the sensitivity and caution required.

Change management fundamentals apply to the organisational purpose, similar to how you would approach a rebranding or a merger. However, changing your organisation's purpose will need you to be on top of your game, more than you would in any other organisational matter.

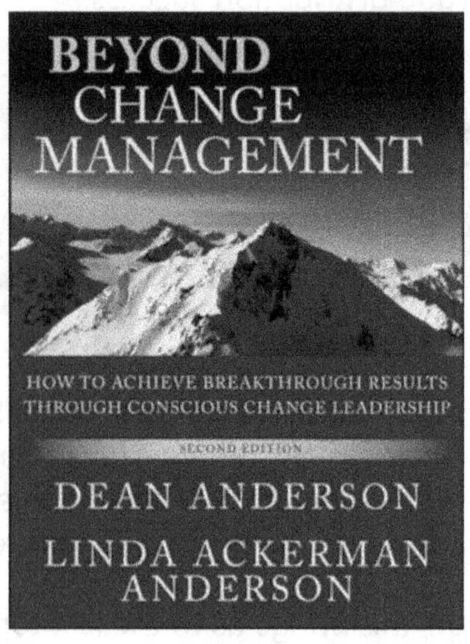

I recommend a delightfully well-written book by Dean Anderson and his wife, Linda Ackerman Anderson, titled Beyond Change Management[6]. More than almost any other book on change that I am aware of, it better illustrates the change processes. They provide 'The Change Leader's Roadmap', which begins with 'Hear the Wake-Up Call'. This step is gold! Because if there is no need to change your organisation's purpose, then don't do it! But if you are 'hearing', or if your continuous, systematic management approach (as prescribed above) is delivering intelligence that necessitates altering your organisation's purpose, you have heard the wake-up call.

---

6 Beyond Change Management | Dean Anderson, Linda Ackerman Anderson - https://www.wiley.com/en-au/Beyond+Change+Management%3A+How+to+Achieve+Breakthrough+Results+Through+Conscious+Change+Leadership%2C+2nd+Edition-p-9780470891131

Then you would need to enter the preparation stage. According to the Anderson's work (or at least my attempt at paraphrasing it), this would include the following:

- Staff the conceived change effort. No living person can alone create, initiate, lead, research, report, design, produce, test, develop, rollout and monitor critical change.
- Create organisational vision, commitment, and capacity. This would involve building organisational understanding of the case for change, developing the vision for change, and creating the change strategy. Then you would need to increase your organisation's capacity to change.
- Assess the situation to determine the design requirements. I see this as taking a quantity surveyor's approach to the change task on hand, estimating what resources will be required.
- Design the desired state. What will it look like? What will it achieve?
- Analyse the impacts. This approach is forward-thinking. It is a careful consideration of who will be impacted. What will be affected? What is the size of the impact? Its upsides and downsides? How long will it take?
- Plan for and organise the implementation phase. Develop an implementation master plan and prepare the organisation to support the implementation.
- Implement the change.
- Celebrate and integrate the new state. Celebrate all the achievements and support the integration and mastery of the new state.
- Learn from and correct the course as necessary. Build systems to continuously improve the new state while learning from your change processes and establishing best practices for future change. Don't forget to dismantle any temporary infrastructures you required during the change process.

If the intended change is incremental, you must determine which recommended transition processes/phases are required. It depends on the desired change's type, size, and impact. A competent change management advisor will provide instruction on the specifics of change implementation. Even a minimal amount of assistance can make the journey easier for you. It requires caution, but there is no need for trepidation.

Changing your organisation's purpose is doable. It requires a solid and intelligent leader with sufficient experience and capacity to steer their team along the necessary change pathways. They must be adequately sensitive to the impacts on People, Processes, Production and Performance. Let me assure you that poorly implemented change of organisational purpose has too many negative consequences to mention in this section, but make no mistake, mismanaged change will cost you, and it will cost you on many levels.

I recommend getting an experienced change advisor to walk you through the process. To be an effective change manager, you need to be more than sufficiently knowledgeable about change management practices; a professional change practitioner is much more than a theorist. They have at least three other qualities; advanced people skills, excellent communications skills, and an inner capacity to genuinely value others.

Within any organisation, a change effect will cause an individual effect; appreciating such impact and, more importantly, caring about it will aid you in becoming more competent as a change manager.

Hopefully, this section has addressed the basics of changing your organisation's purpose sufficiently to assist you when considering the need for any change, your capacity and competency to lead change, the approach to change, the implementation of change and the need to celebrate the change milestones.

Purpose Management Summary

I opened this chapter with the words, *"To start with any other 'P' would be sacrilegious to organisational success!"*

This statement was about the 9P's of **P**urpose, **P**eople, **Processes** (the three core elements), **P**rotection (governance), **P**olicies,

Practices, **P**erformance, **P**roduct and **P**romotion (the six operational elements). I hope you find that I provided a sufficiently substantial and sustained argument to convince you that to start with any 'P' other than Purpose would have been sacrilegious.

Such is the nature and character of organisational purpose. It defines an organisation.

It is:

- *Predictive*; your organisation will become its purpose
- *Addictive*; there is a compulsive engagement in organisational purpose that will drive human behaviour
- *Pecuniary*; it determines your organisation's future security
- *Judicious*; both internal and external stakeholders will judge you by it

It is directed by **inspirational leadership**. It is **sold by vision**. It is **achieved by mission**. Every aspect of an organisation should reflect its purpose. Get it wrong; it will be a career adjustment. Get it right; it will deliver unparalleled professional satisfaction.

I love Purpose: In highly successful organisations, **Purpose reigns! Purpose dominates! Purpose delivers!**

3
PROTECTION MANAGEMENT (GOVERNANCE)

> *"Good corporate governance, it's about being proper and prosper."*
> **Toba Beta**, Author

Having just read nearly thirty pages on the subject of Purpose Management, you are already aware of my position on the subject.

As stated in the previous chapter, "Your organisation's purpose needs to be inspirational. You need a purpose that exudes authenticity, credibility, intentionality, greatness, and value, suggesting inclusion, not exclusion, altruism, not greed. Let us not become delusional here; this is not an easy achievement. It is worth aiming for, nevertheless."

If your organisation has such a purpose, or if you are well advanced in developing it and willing to do whatever it takes to align it to such a purpose, it makes sense to protect it. I refer to this as Protection Management.

Purpose merits Protection

My unshakeable passion for organisational purpose consistently motivates me to stress, at every opportunity, the need to guard your purpose, hence why The Model states that Purpose *merits* Protection.

Along with the digital revolution, many management consultants describe Organisational Governance as the new millennium's growth sector for them. This view might have some contemporary revenue credibility, but the history of governance goes back a long time. For instance, during the Industrial Revolution, the modern patent system was created in France. In 1791 their first comprehensive trademark system was passed into law and spread throughout most western nations by the twentieth century.

However, patents and trademarks are just two of organisations' numerous categories to guard their value and existence.

The Model considers how each of the other five operational Ps benefits from thorough and robust protection. Also, how the organisation's consistently improving governance systems, in turn, help each other operational P.

Every senior manager should (perpetually) be governance mindful and a champion communicator of governance principles and general procedures. Highly successful organisations enjoy a culture of 'living governance', just like its parent element of Purpose; Protection permeates every operational aspect of each division/department.

If you think of Protection as a boat responsible for keeping the organisation afloat, the organisation is one step closer to sinking every time a hole remains unplugged. Most holes are apparent and usually easy to fix, but those tiny and somewhat hidden cracks can be hard to identify and often even more challenging to rectify. Therefore, good Protection Management is critical for your organisation's long-term success.

Applying sound methodologies and developing systems that identify issues, determine solutions, monitor implementation, and review outcomes is the best approach to achieving good governance. It often begins by creating your organisation's bespoke Governance Framework Model.

You can reference many published frameworks as a guide to your approach. Prevalent framework component commonalities for larger organisations include:

- Shareholders
- Board of Directors
- Risk Committee and Nominations Committee
- Finance Committee and Audit Committee
- Filters of Strategic Planning
- Culture
- Value
- Policies
- Delegation of Authorities
- Business Plan
- Business Model Organisational Structure
- Risk Management Framework
- Governance Framework
- Compliance Framework
- Legislation
- External Auditors
- Regional Management Systems
- Operations

The key is to develop a model that meets your organisation's specific dynamics and adapts to future growth or directional change while always complying with relevant legislative matters. While the primary responsibility for governance rests with the Board, senior management must implement and maintain the momentum of effort required to protect the organisation's existence.

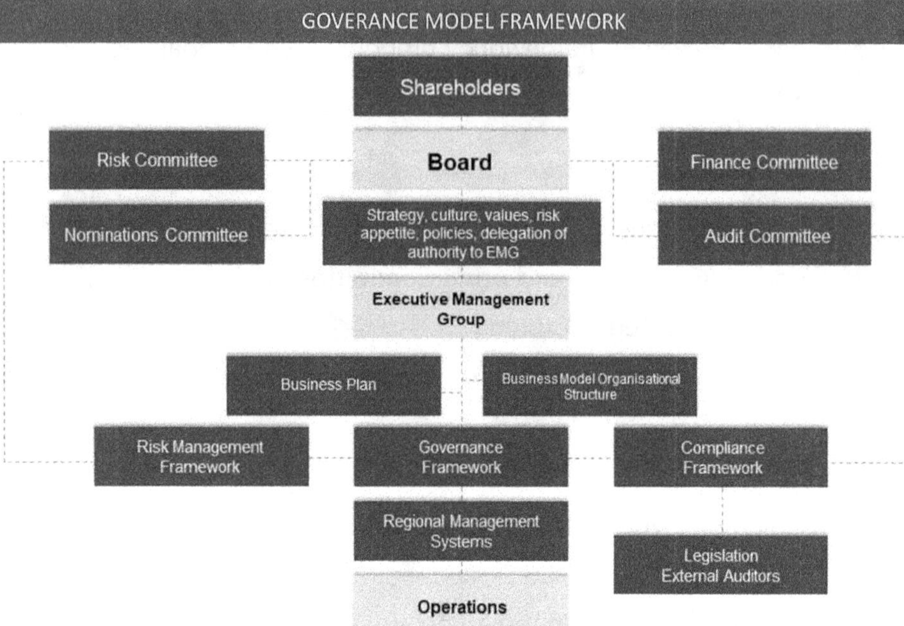

This task becomes easier when there is a complete understanding of the relational impacts that Protection has with its cohort elements. In conjunction with such knowledge, there are real benefits from management being able to articulate, positively, to their staff and other stakeholders as necessary, examples of risk and real-world outcomes of noncompliance. This skill adds to staff's acceptance and confidence that their organisation's Protection is in no way a shallow commitment or just a regulatory 'tick the box' exercise. Naturally, this enhances their sense of job and career security, part of a successful organisation's desired culture.

R.Q. *Just before we dive into considering the relational impacts of Protection to its cohort P's, In your opinion, what gaps exist in your organisation's current governance framework?* ***W.I.D.***

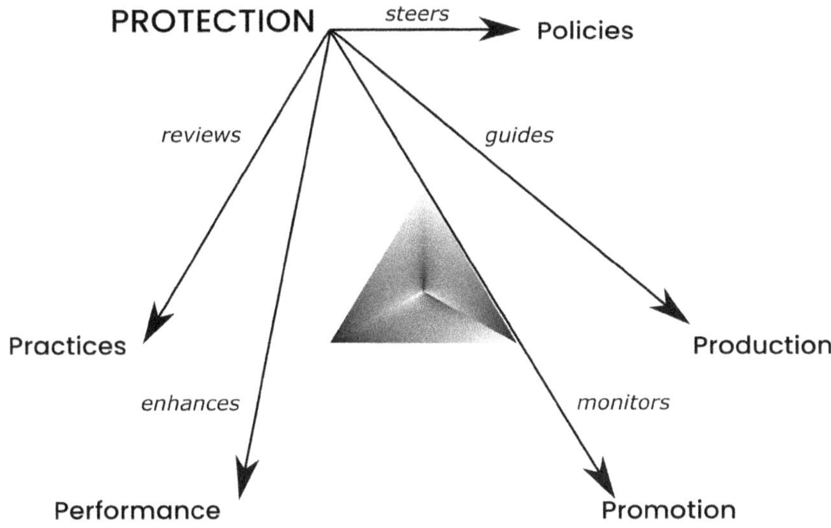

Protection *steers* Policies

Your organisation's Executive Management Group must manage to reflect the stated guidance expressed within the Protection Framework presented by your Board of Directors. It is achieved by well-considered, crafted and implemented policies.

Policies are the actual vehicle by which often intangible organisational governance is delivered. From a Protection perspective, there is some commonality in how successful organisations structure their Policy Frameworks.

Policy Frameworks guide the principles set out in the organisation's Protection Framework, its governing policy, and the essential compliance with ever-changing legislation and regulation. Policy Frameworks usually comprise a model of concise high-level policies and associated procedures, sufficiently detailed, accompanied by various required levels of documentation.

The critical factors of a highly effective Policy Framework lie in the completeness and clarity of the organisation's framework filters; Business Strategy, Values and Culture.

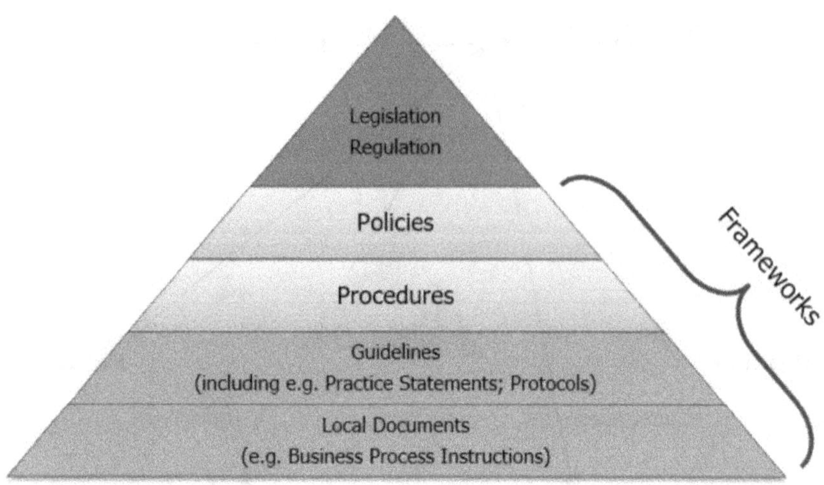

Again, your organisation's Executive Management Group must manage in a way that reflects the stated guidance of your Board of Directors, particularly their Protection Framework's strategies, values, and desired culture. There is no room for management autonomy here.

Best practice dictates that clarity rules. The frameworks of Policies, Procedures, Guidelines and Local Documents must ensure that every person required to read and follow them can easily do so. This standard of refinement causes high levels of compliance that minimise risk and increases productivity through minimising mistakes and redoes. It also adds to the self-esteem of all team members and compliments the 'can do' team culture.

Protection *reviews* Practices

R.Q. *How do you currently review and measure the influence of your organisation's Protection Frameworks on the various workplace practises?* ***W.I.D.***

Humans behave in amazingly unique ways. We are creative, intelligent, responsive, analytical, strategic, explorative, determined, and resilient. We can also be reactive, emotional, self-consumed, indecisive, and sometimes dysfunctional. Our behaviour can vary subject to situational and circumstantial factors, requiring management. We benefit from organisational aspiration and vision (components of Purpose), motivation, inspiration, clear and intentional communication, consistent leadership values, inclusion, appreciation, support, consideration, and reasonable expectation.

The world is changing, just as our language, qualities and practices inside the working environment are evolving. Equally, the scope, intent, design, depth, delivery, review, improvement, and sturdiness of Protection Management are all changing. The quest for people-centred organisations and ethical conduct must continue. Having guidelines and limits around what is and is not suitable gives everyone a sense of security at work.

Aspirational excellence within your organisation requires a continual commitment to development, delivery, assessment, and Protection review. Mature Protection frameworks evaluate human practices, delivering (a form of) risk insurance and a platform for practice improvement. Additionally, as stated near the beginning of this chapter, mature Protection provides a sense of job and career security. In the later chapter on People management, we remember Abraham Maslow's theory on the hierarchy of human needs. In most western nations, only having employment satisfies the minimum level of security, only the bare necessities.

Highly successful organisations want and deliver much more than the basics. They expect their people to experience more than their psychological needs of belongingness and esteem. They are committed to providing self-fulfilment, the self-actualisation of achieving one's potential.

Remember my underlying mantra: *A worthy & defined Purpose delivered by valued People utilising highly developed Processes = organisational success leading to sustainable excellence!* In the context of Protection *reviews* Practices, the keywords of my belief statement are '**valued People**'. If you believe you have good people committed to a great purpose, contributing decent ideas and proficient effort, they deserve superior Protection. One vital factor here is the ownership of the detail and practicalities of such

Protection. Including your people in your Protection portfolio's developing and review phases, will deliver a measurably higher attainable standard of governance and enhance broader Purpose ownership.

While having outstanding Protection is just one of the factors that cause such success, it remains essential to achieving the desired organisational culture discussed throughout this book.

Protection *enhances* Performance

In a comprehensive joint white paper by Deloitte – Nyenrode Research Program[7] investigating the relationship between good governance and corporate performance, they concluded that good governance leads to high performance.

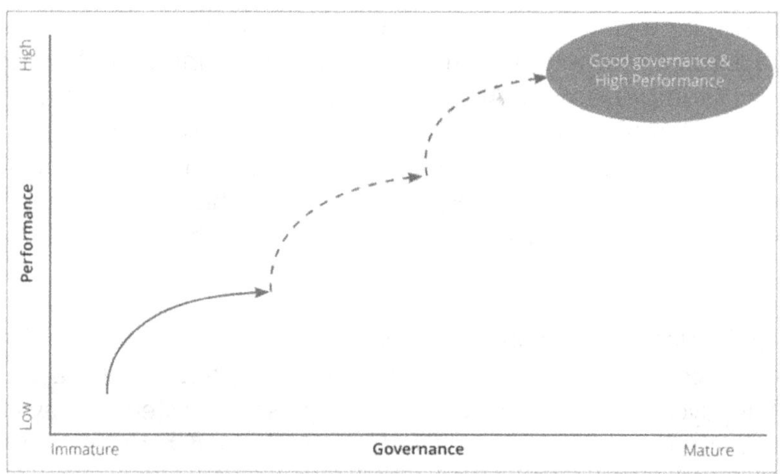

"Our research results support the hypothesis that good governance enhances corporate performance, as it produces six governance variables with an academically proven positive impact on performance. These identified 'good' governance variables are board independence, board diversity, remuneration, CEO

7 Governance & Corporate Performance | Deloitte - Nyenrode Research Program - https://www2.deloitte.com/content/dam/Deloitte/nl/Documents/risk/deloitte-nl-risk-good-governance-driving-corporate-performance.pdf

characteristics, oversight and ownership structure. Conclusive evidence has found that each of these variables can enhance corporate performance, but there is no one size fits all approach to applying them in practice."

This meta-analysis research confirms my long-held view that Protection enhances Performance. I studied the white paper, and many 'take-aways' highlighted the logical relationship between good governance and high performance.

Following is one abstract that should be of interest to every senior manager:

> "There are several schools of thought describing the dynamics of corporate governance. Most scholars use the agency theory, but stewardship theory and stakeholder theory are also used to explain the dynamics between the different stakeholders in a company. These three theories are not mutually exclusive or collectively exhaustive, but they provide fundamental explanations to many of the findings in our research into governance and performance.
>
> **Agency theory**
>
> Agency theory assumes the core friction is the conflict of interests between the different parties involved in the company. An agency problem exists if a principal, such as a shareholder, employs an agent, such as the CEO and executive team, to lead the company on the principal's behalf. Agency theory assumes that managers and shareholders are expected to have potentially conflicting interests.
>
> *Following agency theory, corporate governance, in the form of rule setting, monitoring and incentive and sanctioning mechanisms, is needed to align the interests.*
>
> **Stakeholder theory**
>
> Stakeholder theory assumes the core friction is that the good performance of companies depends on the contributions of many different parties. These stakeholders – shareholders as well as other parties - all have a stake in the company and can

choose how to prioritize their stakes based on the information they have about the company. It is the responsibility of the management to balance all these interests. At the same time, the stakeholders will try to influence management to meet their interests, goals and expectations.

Following stakeholder theory, corporate governance is needed to make sure that the voice of stakeholders is heard and that information about the company is distributed equally to all stakeholders.

Stewardship theory

Stewardship theory assumes that management should put the long-term best interest of a group ahead of the individual's self-interest. Stewards, unlike agents in the agency theory, consider their interests to be aligned with the interests of the corporation and its shareholders. In addition, managers as stewards are in the best position to maximize the interests of stakeholders, including shareholders, since they are most familiar with the dynamics of corporate strengths, weaknesses, opportunities, and threats.

According to the stewardship theory, corporate governance in the form of selecting and training competent and trustworthy managers is required to commit all parties to work towards a common goal without taking advantage of each other."

The above work by Deloitte – Nyenrode Research Program[8] underpins numerous other credible sources dedicated to research and professional services delivery, including:

- The Australian Institute of Company Directors (AICD) key governance report[9], and

8 Governance Theories | Deloitte - Nyenrode Research Program - https://www2.deloitte.com/content/dam/Deloitte/nl/Documents/risk/deloitte-nl-risk-good-governance-driving-corporate-performance.pdf

9 Key Governance Report | Australian Institute of Company Directors (AICD) - https://aicd.companydirectors.com.au/-/media/cd2/resources/advocacy/governance-leadership-centre/pdf/kay-governance-report-whitepaper-report.ashx

- Global Professional Services firm Grant Thornton, in their corporate governance and company performance paper[10].

Protection *guides* Production

Production comes in all shapes and types; items manufactured, services delivered, physical, virtual, and cyber. Most organisations produce multiple products. The guidance relationship between Protection and Production can be direct and/or indirect. While People → Practices *shape* (invent, design, create and deliver) Production, the sustainable lifetime of your production and its profitability depend on the quality of your organisation's Protection.

History is unkind to organisations that have sold products that have not aligned with their organisation's strategies, culture, and values, either at their invention stage or after making materially altering changes. Protection's Business Plan, Risk Management Framework, and Compliance Framework are three components that tangibly *guide* Production.

10 Corporate Governance and Performance | https://www.grantthornton.co.uk/globalassets/1.-member-firms/united-kingdom/pdf/documents/corporate-governance-and-company-performance.pdf

Do not undervalue or handle Protection's impact on Production loosely. There needs to be transparent respect for Protection's authority and contribution. This respect is a top-down management priority, making all team members aware of the organisation's 'Protection *guides* Production' ethos. Product Development (PD) frameworks have progressed significantly in recent years. There is now a raft of consulting firms specialising in this space, providing advice, templates and tools for building robust PD frameworks tailored to suit your organisation. I particularly liked the approach taken by Roman Pichler[11] in his framework presented here.

---

11 Product Development Framework | Roman Pichler - https://www.romanpichler.com/blog/romans-product-management-framework/

Protection *monitors* Promotion

R.Q. *When you read the word promotion, what immediately comes to mind?* ***W.I.D.***

Every Product needs Promotion. Promotion directly links to profitability, perhaps more than any other operational P element. Yet, many examples of organisations suffered because they allowed the product's promotion to become out of alignment with the organisation's purpose, culture, and values.

The Model has carefully identified Promotion as a Processes P since Processes *deploy* Promotion. Because of the requisite creative and enthusiastic nature promoters possess, it is the one P that requires constant review; Promotion *yields* to Protection.

I have observed that in highly successful organisations, Promotion begins long before advertising optics are required and before briefing marketing representatives. It starts by internally testing the perceived need for your product. This step will require some visionary narrative. Before undertaking substantial development, an optimum outcome is having as many of your people as possible sold on the concept.

Once the vast majority of your team is on board, that organisation-wide internal optimism will fuel the external Promotion. It will also increase the level of Protection because genetics come into play. Promotion becomes a product of your values and culture.

While Protection's primary relational impact with Promotion is monitoring, Promotion also benefits from the directives of Protection's Risk Management Framework through its compliance framework.

Protection Management Summary

This chapter is in no way a definitive work on Protection Management. The topic of Protection Management (particularly its treatment within The Model) deserves to be a stand-alone book, as does each of its cohort operational elements; Policies, Practices, Performance, Production and Promotion. This chapter describes the fundamentals of Protection Management and its fit in The Model.

I included examples of the essential frameworks and research proofs as a guide to the basics of governance. I hope you agree that Purpose *merits* Protection and that Protection (Governance) deserves a considerable investment in development and improvement.

Unfortunately, or perhaps thankfully, there is no 'off the shelf, one suits all' package that will satisfy your organisation's requirement for a secure and effective Protection Management program. Your organisation's purpose is worthy of a tailormade Protection Management solution. There is a considerable offering of professional assistance in the marketplace for those who have not had a reasonable engagement with Protection Management or are about to be responsible for it.

Nevertheless, let me encourage you not to become anxious or overwhelmed by the thought of being responsible for driving Protection Management within your organisation. It is a logical construct of understandable steps. Follow the established and proven processes found to construct your chosen frameworks and seek assistance when necessary from professional advisors or consultants (depending on your specific needs). You will soon become familiar with the purpose requirements and best governance practices. These familiarities will be further enhanced by successfully applying The Model's Relational Factors in your development and ongoing tuning of your organisation's Protection Management. You will begin operating from The P9 Management Model paradigm, which will beneficially affect how you think and approach future decision-making.

Protection Management is the first operational element of The Model to be explored, understood, valued, and applied. It has also set this book's structural style and tone for its five remaining operational elements.

4

POLICIES MANAGEMENT

> *"Our differences are policies; our agreements, principles."*
> **William McKinley**, 25th president of the United States

Purpose *drives* Policies

The P9 Management Model contends that Policies are a 'Purpose P' because "Purpose *drive* Policies and Policies *reflect* Protection". It is the protection that your organisation's purpose deserves. Developing and maintaining an organisation-wide understanding and genuine appreciation of this heightens the position and respect of policies within your organisation.

This acknowledgement and respect of policies aid in building, developing and fine-tuning The Model's styled culture in your organisation that you desire.

A policy's primary objective is to be a guiding principle that achieves the intended outcome of its creator/s.

Highly successful organisations cautiously, strategically and thoroughly develop new policies and review existing policies.

"Can a Policy exist without being written"? Yes, it can be legally and practically, but I quickly point out that it is a minimal practice in highly successful organisations. Applying the common-sense test is best when there is a justification for unwritten policies. Do this in a manner that makes the reason for having such a policy transparently obvious, e.g. public announcement, *riding your bike in the aisles of this aeroplane is prohibited.*

Discretionary unwritten policies are open to misinterpretation, inconsistency, and abuse, both by the enforcer and the recipient user. Unwritten policies can undermine the desired culture of excellence, which causes unwanted outcomes, including uncertainty, concern, indifference, disrespect, and even insubordination.

For a policy to be highly effective, it needs the following **preferred qualities**:

- Intent: it must have a clear purpose and the backing of senior management
- Stature: it is enforceable
- Inclusive: its scope includes all relevant users
- Rationale: it needs to make sense to its users
- Relevance: it needs to be appropriate to its users and position within the organisation
- Achievable: it can be (effectively) implemented
- Pliable: it can accommodate future changes
- Cultural: it fits well in the organisation's culture

As you would expect, depending on the purpose and scope of a policy, there will also be varying complexity required across the broad range of policies that you will create and maintain within your organisation. Indeed this is another opportunity to apply the KIS principle. A concise and clear introductory description of the policy's intent will significantly assist your team members in understanding it, accepting it, and their required compliance with it. This information forms part of The Model's desired culture in that it builds an enhanced level of respect and trust in your organisation's leadership and senior management.

Alternatively, policies that are any of the following:

- Abstract or Unnecessary
- Not easily understood
- Not clear as to the expectation
- Seemingly overcomplicated
- Unreasonably challenging to comply with
- Unfair, biased or prejudice

will lead to unfortunate, unnecessary, unintended, and undesired counter-productive outcomes.

At a macro level, the method of recording you utilise for managing the broad range of policies created and maintained within your organisation is essential. This task is measurably easier for a start-up entity than for a long-established organisation that has never correctly catalogued its policies. A well-designed, practical, and user-friendly Policy register is an essential component for an organisation that aims to be exceptional.

Design

As with Protection Management, various models and easily accessible frameworks exist for creating a policy. Many of them have a top-down structure (tiers) of hierarchical status, like this example from the NSW Government[12], which answers the initial questions people ask about policy formation

12 Policy Development Framework | NSW Government - https://www.digital.nsw.gov.au/article/whats-name-deconstructing-and-defining-policy

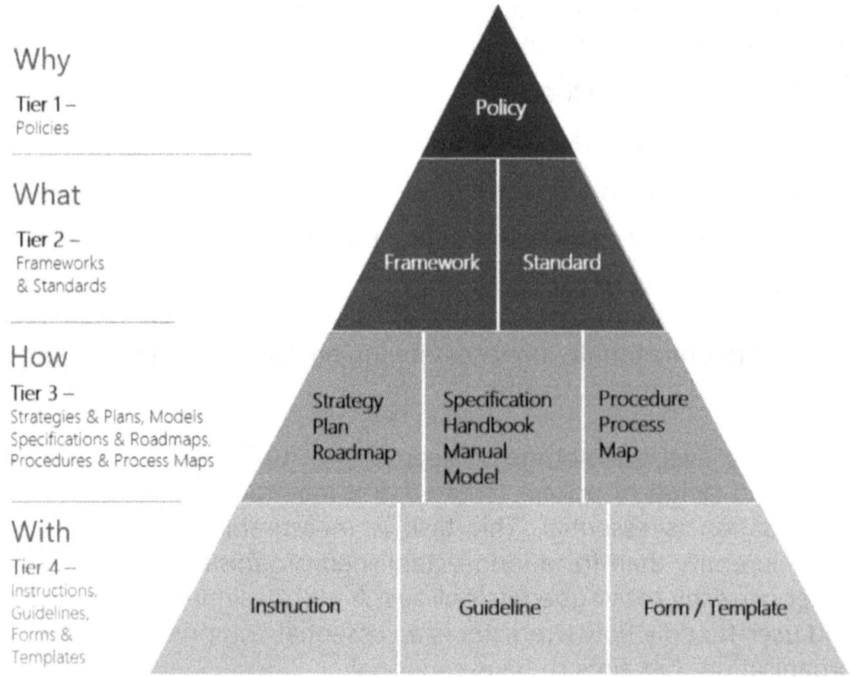

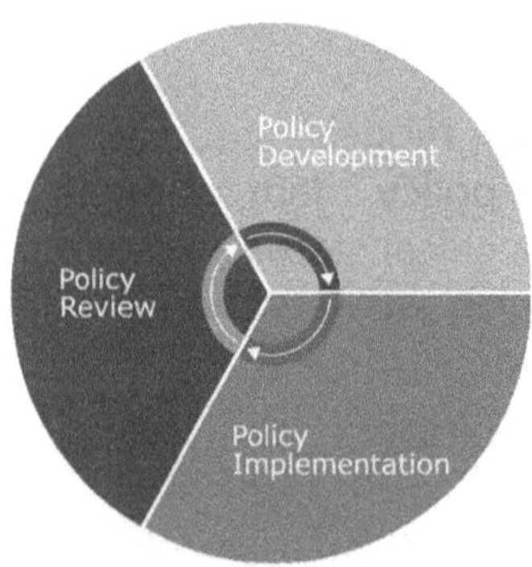

You may not consider that the level of sophistication illustrated in the above framework is necessary for your organisation. Still, by understanding its contents and intent, you might choose to cherry-pick and/or combine certain aspects in developing your organisation's framework. My experience is that even in a small business or NFP entity, adopting a considered and systematic method for policy design, implementation and management will pay excellent and long-lasting returns on your investment of time and resources.

R.Q. *Are you satisfied with your organisation's current Policies Management? If there are flaws, what are they?* ***W.I.D.***

Implementation and Management

In the example framework above, Tier 4 deals with the implementation and management aspects. Tier 1 is about the purpose and need of the policy, while Tiers 2 and 3 are primarily the design tiers.

Tier 4 is the 'where the rubber meets the road' tier. You have invested time carefully planning and drafting the directional components (Tiers 2 &3), ensuring that they meet the intended purpose of the policy. It is now time to create the user engagement components. A good starting point is determining the sophistication and detail required to achieve the policy's intent.

Referring to the 'preferred qualities' list provided above can significantly assist in deciding the required and reasonable level of sophistication needed. There needs to be an ample and appropriate amount of time and resources invested in the policy implementation phase to ensure a thorough understanding of and compliance with the policy.

The goal here is to have a good policy. There is not a good way to implement a bad policy, and a mediocre policy design is a common cause of experiencing a poor implementation phase. Furthermore, a well-designed policy can be poorly implemented, so it is wise to continually consider policy implementation throughout the (policy) development phase.

So, the stated intent of the policy, desired outcomes, predetermined priorities, and step-by-step actions must be sufficiently clear during the policy development process to ensure that all end-users can correctly and consistently interpret and implement them successfully. Consequently, the quantity and quality of occurring communication play a critical role in facilitating the policy's successful implementation.

Highly successful organisations approach this need by:

- Including, from the start, communication methods and frequencies to ensure that throughout every phase
- Information is adequately shared

- Feedback is not only sought; it is valued and acted upon (promptly)
- Rectifying problems promptly
- Always celebrating wins

The timing and context for policy implementation need to be on the essential checklist. Many other implementation efforts may co-exist in different parts of your organisation when implementing a new or materially changed policy. The key here is coherence, which can help create a climate for implementation success.

Once a policy is implemented and operating, You move into the management phase.

Another recommended step is to ensure that adequate, user-friendly feedback mechanisms are established between the line management and end-users upon implementation to ensure that the policy is as intended and addresses any unanticipated consequences efficiently.

Policy Development and Policy Implementation are (often) distinct stages within a policy cycle. The line between Policy Development and Policy Implementation can become quite blurred.

It is good practice to consider the policy's implementation as an integral feature of the policy development stage. Wherever possible, involve policy creators and end-users in the entire policy cycle process.

In my experience, policy initiatives are more effective when designed with direct end-user input. Policy creators may not have had relevant training or direct knowledge regarding the policy's intent. End-users provide a real-world perspective on the feasibility of a particular policy initiative.

Reviews Management

Reviews are to improvement what fertilizer is to a garden; not compulsory but highly recommended. It is also true that no sensible sailor would take off from one port to travel over a considerable distance to a predetermined destination without regularly checking their charts. So it is in the ocean of commercial activity where the currents of expectation compete with the winds of obstructions.

Intelligent organisations commit to Review Management; they realise the benefits of scheduled analytical exercises that are planned and purposeful. A good review will be the product of a good review process, established and proven to work. Review management is logical and achievable for all organisations, irrespective of size. As a practice, it should be performed in such a manner to ensure that all key user stakeholders value it within an organisation.

An objective review, sufficiently scoped, should identify misalignment and make detailed recommendations for policy amendments and procedural modifications. Do not underestimate the usefulness and positive results of performing analytically structured and appropriately scheduled policy reviews.

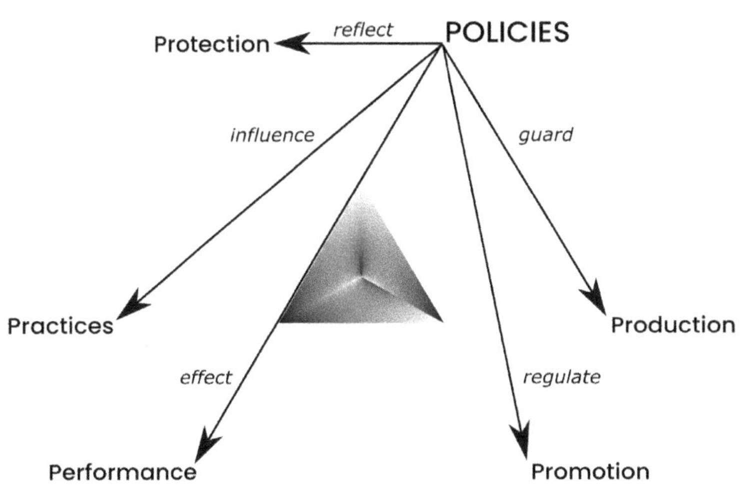

Policies *reflect* Protection

I previously wrote, "it is your organisation's Executive Management Group (or a general manager in a smaller business) that must manage in such a way that reflects the stated guidance of your Board of Directors Protection Framework". So to be consistent with that, it is logical to argue that Policies must *reflect* Protection.

Again, using the example framework above and aligning it to the core elements of The Model:

- Tier 1, the WHY, is the Purpose focused tier
- Tiers 2, the WHAT, and 3, the HOW, are both People focused tiers
- Tier 4, the WITH, is the Processes tier

WHY: A policy's primary objective is to be a guiding principle that achieves the intended outcome. Having decided that a policy is necessary, wanted, and beneficial, it is vital to realise that it must still align with your **organisation's** purpose and desired **culture**. A policy that users could consider counter-culture or misaligned to (their understanding of) the organisation's stated purpose will have unnecessary and unfortunate consequences.

Make sure you answer the following **WHY questions**. Why is this policy needed? Why now? Why is management confident that it will work? Why, as the end-user, should I be satisfied with the practicality and the intended achievement of this new policy? Predetermining your answers to such questions can dramatically impact the implementation phase of a new policy.

When designing a new policy with legislative or external regulatory compliance considerations, ensure that you include all necessary players (internal and external) in the process.

WHAT: When considering what frameworks might best suit and what will be the necessary standards, their formality and the subsequent intensity of compliance necessary to meet and maintain the established core standards acceptably (e.g. security, safety, professionalism and sustainable excellence), you must contemplate the skill sets and mindsets of the intended users, and anticipate their likely responsive behaviour and applied methods.

This approach is, of course, only valid if the users of your policy are not robots.

Also needing consideration is that there may be synergies with or divergence from other policies or strategies within your organisation. Policies may interact with each other, producing new, unplanned and occasionally unintended consequences. More complex governance and accountability provisions may be required to administer the policy implementation.

HOW: Because People *perform* Practices and People *determine* Performance, consider carefully the design of the facilities, methods and tools to be used, and the approach required during the roll-out phase. This tactic is another good reason to involve end-users from the beginning wherever possible. Here is an opportunity to explain the facilities, methods, tools, and required approach.

WITH: So, the Why, What, and How combine to form the chassis of a potentially high-performance vehicle, but it is the body that the drivers and passengers engage with, meaning this WITH tier is the tier where detail, clarity, practicality, effective delivery, and the measure of acceptance and compliance occurs.

I hope you agree that maintaining a purpose-driven approach to policy preparation is critical.

Remember the value of your organisation's purpose (which *drives* policies) and your wise investment in its Protection (governance) platform. This mindset ensures that the specific new policy you are now responsible for implementing and managing *reflects* the Protection platform accurately, strengthening and securing your organisation's purpose.

Policies *influence* Practices

It does not take long for someone new in a management role to recognise the impacts of policy amendments on an individual's behaviour and actions (Practices) when required to comply with such modifications. Users will demonstrate the policy's practical impact from highly negative to strongly positive when asked.

Have you ever noticed that when staff consider a policy illogical, punitive or burdensome, they can promptly personalise and internalise their feelings and opinions? Yet, when policies are perceived to be:

- Logical
- Achievable
- Beneficial

the default thinking of staff becomes externalised, pragmatic, acceptive and supportive.

If policies are perceived to be or are punitive or burdensome, then the response will likely be one of the following:

- Frustration
- A sense of not being considered and of being undervalued
- A sense of being offended
- Reluctance
- Rejection (no buy-in)
- Disgust and irreverence

When perceived as logical, achievable and beneficial, policies will generally be quickly accepted and considered appropriate.

Beyond a new policy's reaction and implementation period, the relationship reflecting 'Policies *influencing* Practices' should be consistently apparent. Policies *influence* Practices, and Practices *impact* Performance, not just the performance of production, but your overall organisational performance.

This reality is why policy creation and development must be purpose-driven for your organisation to become exceptional. Not just purpose considered and sensitive, but purpose centric, ensuring that the policy's cause, intent, implementation, and ongoing management are consistent with your organisation's core values and declared purpose. This approach is another way your organisation's purpose can continually permeate the atmosphere and influence your entire organisation's culture.

A short note of caution. A dilution of the desired alignment between policies and the organisation's purpose, and Protection, will occur when someone (particularly at the middle management level) new to the organisation (and not fully aware of the culture and standards) makes amendments. This occurrence is evident even in well-managed and high-performing organisations that apply best practice policy management. To avoid this and similarly problematic experiences, the investment of time and the quality content in your staff induction sessions minimises that likelihood. It also minimises the time it takes to fully have the new team member on board with the culture and perform to the desired competencies and outcomes.

Policies *affect* Performance

The P9 Management Model declares a clear and logical pathway in stating that 'People *perform* Practices' and 'People *determine* Performance'. Following The Model's position that Policies *influence* the Practices that People carry out only substantiates the conclusion that Policies *affect* Performance.

How performance is affected, and to the degree of any effect, will vary significantly depending upon numerous factors, including the policy's nature, breadth, complexity, staff safety, and security implications. Consequently, give attentive and considerable care to the policy's intent, creation, implementation, amendments, management, and reviews.

We are all aware of the statement that "human beings are creatures of habit", and you will find sufficient studies to support that saying. It is often the case that even when individuals think there might be a better way of achieving a particular task, they continue to use their long-practised procedures. Studies of such incidents have identified reasons including:

- They feel comfortable

- It is easier
- they consider amendments or significant changes risky

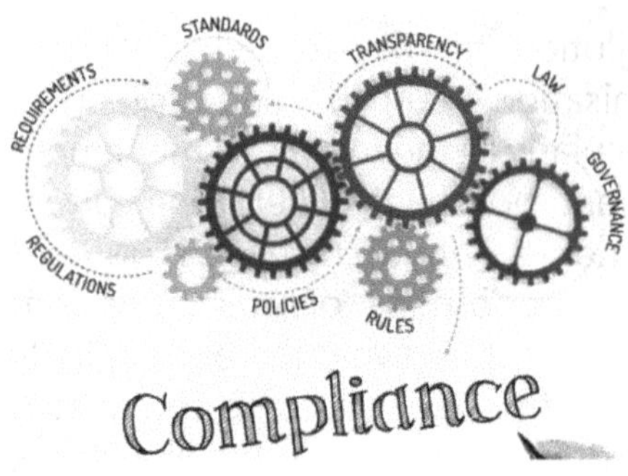

You can counter new policy reluctance. When introducing a new policy, it is wise to invest time by creating a well-thought-out and prepared narrative that includes answers to the 'WHY questions' proposed in the Policies *reflect* Protection section above. Also, when introducing a new policy, referring to two or three other current and widely known policies recognised and celebrated for their success can be advantageous.

People *determine* Performance, and Policies *affect* Performance. Because of this, the more logical it is to have end-user/beneficiary representation present at all phases of the policy cycle, ensuring that you give due consideration to real-world practicalities.

Only having the end-user/beneficiary included in the review phase has been an unfortunate and disappointing observation I have regularly made throughout my consultancy years. The resulting poor performance was not an operative issue but a design issue. You can avoid this by having end-user/beneficiary representation in the design phase. On other occasions, it was an operative and design issue that could have been avoided by having end-user/beneficiary representation included throughout the cycle.

Over time, your staff gain confidence knowing that their organisation is purpose-driven, well-led and managed, committed to its core values, and inclusive of all necessary players. This knowledge and experience encourage staff to be proactive in identifying and presenting current or foreseen issues and proposing corrective or alternate solutions.

Policies *guard* Production

Every organisation produces things. Some of those things are tangible, while others are intangible. The focus of policy attention might be administrative, promotional or managerial, all requiring relevant procedures and policies. Some organisations are service-focused, while others are product-focused. Most things that an organisation produces are not the end product. Instead, they are either incremental items required to assist in or to include in creating the end product.

One good example is the procedures used to produce the end product. Not every procedure requires or benefits from having ownership of its unique policy. They will likely be part of a technical manual or instruction list. Best practice methodology constructs an umbrella policy. Or, depending on the item, size, complexity, and intent of the processed tasks, numerous policies will provide direction, minimum expectations, and requirements, including quality, safety, responsibility, accountability levels, and cultural compatibility.

If a separate policy, the primary purpose of that policy will be any or all of the following:

- To *guard:*
    - The end product's performance
    - The product's reputation
    - The organisation's reputation
    - The product's longevity and sales volume
- To *guard* the organisation's investment in the product's process, including I.T., I.P., equipment and infrastructure facilities.

To achieve sustainable excellence, the policy cycle as part of Policy Management is another area in the daily life of your organisation. You can significantly impact organisational performance by applying The Model's approach of considering each P element when creating or amending a policy.

Policies *regulate* Promotion

"Without promotion, something terrible happens... nothing!" is a famous quote by P.T. Barnum (1810 - 1891), founder of Barnum & Bailey Circus. He was a showman, a businessman, and a politician. It is a simple and timely reminder of the importance of promotion to all of us. Still, unfettered or misaligned promotion can constrain the potential success of your product; it can also damage your organisation's hard-earned reputation.

The two consistent activities of promotion are sales and marketing. These can cover both internal and external targets. You can achieve these activities with human engagement or other modes, including digital, print, banners, sponsorships, etc. Irrespective of the delivery mode, continual (daily) good management is critical.

The Promotion element of The Model is perhaps one of the most obvious targets for the need for sound policy development, implementation, management and review. It is also the leading element for the two primary aspects of regulation; settings and control.

The nature of promotion requires individuals to be creative and explore new frontiers. While these attributes need to be acknowledged, encouraged and retained, policies also contain and can execute authoritative control when:

- Content is unacceptable or incorrect, or
- Overly ambitious or misaligned promotional activities occur, or
- When considered that they crossed the line of the policy settings or are aggressively non-compliant

Policies Management Summary

A policy has three responsibilities:

1. To achieve a purpose that solves a problem or satisfies a need
2. To provide clear direction and guidance

3. To be a final, authoritative point of reference demanding compliance

Winston Churchill once said that *"The price of greatness is responsibility".*

Management is a privilege that comes with status, reward, and the burden of responsibility for successfully managing your organisation's portfolio of policies. To achieve this success, you must ensure the result of a policy's development, implementation, and reviews achieve the policy's purpose and contribute to, and align with, your organisation's purpose.

An inconsistent policy or a policy diverging from your organisation's purpose will be detrimental to the desired culture and overall organisational performance. A policy that causes tension between it and another policy or opposes another policy damages cohesive operations. Hence, you need to optimise all the best practice requirements outlined above by adopting an ongoing P9 Management style and approach to the Policy Cycle and the Policy Register.

Beyond good management, there needs to be good leadership at all levels of policy management. Effective leadership is required to shape and reshape mandates, provide resources, structures, and, where necessary, programmes that underwrite good policies.

The necessary promoted mindset and approach for the type of leader that The Model attracts acquires a thorough understanding of the impact of sound policies on all the organisation's stakeholders. They particularly appreciate how providing effective policy management helps achieve their goal. The goal of every team member has a sense of validation. This outcome is because:

- Of their experience of not only being informed of each policy's WHY, WHAT, HOW, and WITH factors
- Having gratification for and confidence in the knowledge that there is appropriate and inclusive representation included in each phase of the policy cycle

- Having respect for their organisation's capacity to maintain a well-performing and easily accessed policy register will educate them on a policy's intent, answer questions, clarify misunderstandings, and identify potential or actual policy conflicts or divergence

> **R.Q.** *What is your opinion on how well those last three bullet points regarding Protection Management reflect the daily reality for most of your workforce?* ***W.I.D.***

Again I will state that The Model contends that Policies are a 'Purpose P' because "Purpose *drives* Policies and Policies *reflect* Protection", the protection your organisation's Purpose deserves. Simply put, Policies become the governance vehicle that Protection uses to achieve the strategic plan that will deliver the objectives of your organisation's purpose.

5

PEOPLE MANAGEMENT

> *"It is good people who make good places."*
> **Anna Sewell,** Author

R.Q. *When considering People management, what do you believe are the philosophies and practices of highly successful organisations?* ***W.I.D.***

Alignment

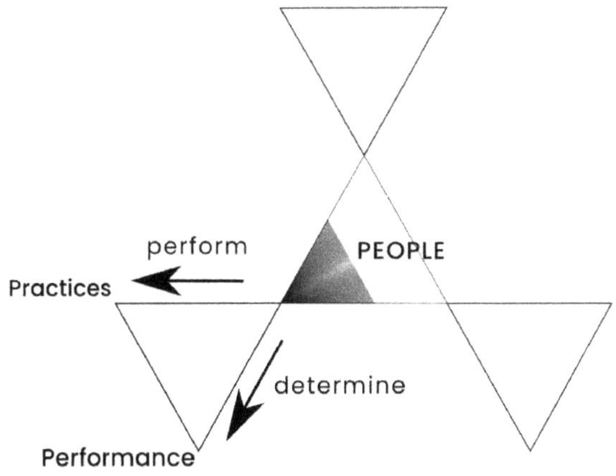

As one of the three core elements of The P9 Management Model, it is critically important that you embrace all the vital aspects of People Management. Its two cohort elements are Practises and Performance. Competently overseeing People Management is essential for fully accomplishing your organisation's exceptional performance targets and sustainable excellence objectives.

When the opportunity arises, one question I like to ask mid-level managers is, *what is the purpose of your organisation employing people?* Their answers often highlight a distinct disconnect between their organisation's vision statement and their view of employees.

Highly successful organisations look at their people through the value lens. They see their people as intrinsically valuable, not only for what they produce but also for what they contribute. Such language is not just another cliché. Instead, it is apparent in the quality and enthusiasm of their staff, how they train and treat their team, and by observing the organisation's strategic culture of mutual respect.

Single employee organisations have their place but are rarely renowned for being highly successful. Whether or not you consider yourself a 'people person', as a senior manager, one of your primary views should be to recognise your need for good people, your people, your team members.

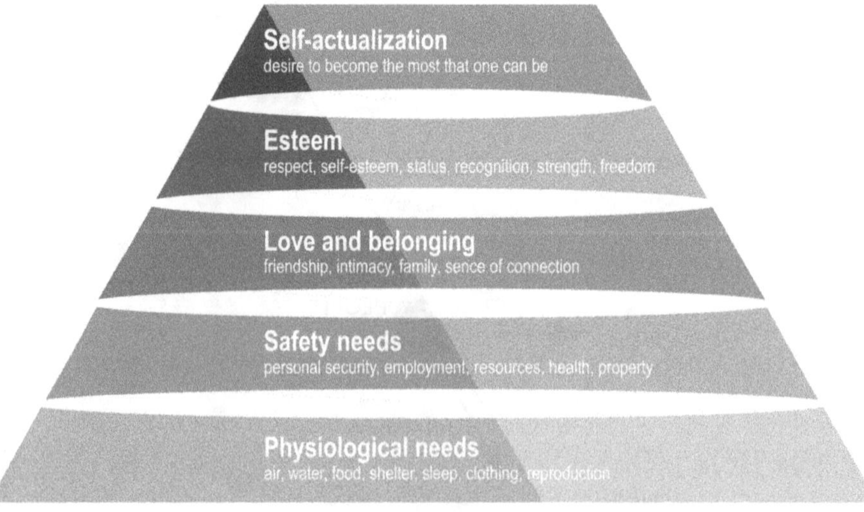

I imagine you are familiar with Maslow's hierarchy of human needs, commonly considered the most recognised theory, but here is a reminder of its details.

Its lower two levels address an individual's basic needs, the lowest being biological & physiological, then safety.

Its middle two levels address psychological needs: love/belonging, then esteem.

But its highest level addresses one's self-fulfilment needs.

Senior management of highly successful organisations willingly work hard to create an environment in which every team member can and will want to become their best, fulfil their personal goals, and enjoy the consequential rewards. There must be more than words spoken at the scheduled performance reviews or on workplace motivational posters. It must be a top-down commitment to providing an atmosphere of mutual respect, individual value, expectation and appreciation of high contribution levels, and encouragement for every individual to improve and grow. Numerous examples of highly successful organisations using this approach reveal that it creates 'can do' teams, comprising individuals who experience working in a 'no idea is stupid' ethos with the resulting tangible benefits of productivity and stimulus.

In an organisation of many people, what individuals do and how they do it affects the entire organisation. Practices fuel culture. What individuals and groups do, and how they do it, determines the lifestyle of an organisation! I like how **American Councils for International Education** illustrate and address organisational culture in the following extract:

The following is part of a presentation by Deloitte Insights[13] that articulates the relationship between culture and strategy well.

"The two are connected. When a company's culture is aligned with business strategy, it attracts people who feel comfortable in it, which in turn should produce a high level of engagement. Conversely, programs to improve engagement often discover cultural issues, forcing the company and its leadership to question and change its values, incentives, programs, and structure. Both culture and engagement require CEO-level commitment and strong support from HR to understand, measure, and improve."

Your organisation's culture should greatly interest you as a senior manager. The culture of your organisation did not occur

---

13 Organisational Culture | Deloitte Insights - https://www2.deloitte.com/us/en/insights/focus/human-capital-trends/2016/impact-of-culture-on-business-strategy.html

accidentally. It is a product of leadership and management. It takes proactive participation and a systematic investment of your time, requiring you to identify and assess current aspects that you believe do not align with your desired culture. It would be best if you regularly thought of the what, how, and when to introduce change.

I observed that all the organisations I have studied had a strong culture, but not all were intentional or desirable. Consequently, I believe CEOs should write their own Workplace Culture Statement, which is an excellent partner to the organisation's Purpose Statement. A Workplace Culture Statement firstly makes the CEO think about what type of environment will best deliver the objectives of the Purpose Statement, and secondly, how to implement it. Using the 'Components of Purpose' philosophy as a guide, presented in the chapter on Purpose Management, will help you develop a valuable Workplace Culture Statement. Having your P&C (HR) Director on board early in the process will be wise, but it remains essential for you, as the CEO, to own it. Also, a P&C Director who is on board with the intent of the organisation's Purpose Statement and its Workplace Culture Statement will approach many of their responsibilities through these documents, particularly staff selection criteria.

Employee turnover is a high cost for every organisation. Research constantly shows that for highly trained staff, recruitment, induction, training, and associated production downtime, can cost more than 200% of the annual salary of such a person. Similar research highlights that mid-level managers can falsely attribute employee turnover to the quantity of marketplace job offers or claim the employee was not a correct job fit. However, direct research with employees who recently exited their position shows a vast majority left because of their manager. This situation can be because of a straightforward issue with their manager or a variety of secondary reasons caused by managers.

Because people are different, they naturally behave, think, communicate, react, and perform differently. Most average organisations write specifications for every role their staff perform (Job Descriptions). The next step for an organisation desiring to improve its performance is to create a Job Profile for the position, which typically would include a preferred aptitude level and behavioural style. Another step for highly successful organisations distinguishes them; they profile the preferred **behavioural style for each team** (a TBP – Team Behavioural Profile) within their organisation. Their management style is a predetermined view of what a specific team will do and when.

Many tools are available to assist an organisation in determining, designing, and processing the above. Here are a few examples of credible firms in that space:

- DISC
- DNA Behavior
- Herrmann Brain Dominance Instrument
- Keirsey Temperament Sorter
- Myers-Briggs Type Indicator

Using such a process is a sophisticated approach to recruiting members to a respected and well-developed team, and it is an established method for getting good results. It does not mean every team member will have the same behavioural style. It is also improbable that it would be required or desirable. Teams need different behavioural types to complement each other and contribute from their individualities. Establish your preferred team profile and select individuals whose preferred aptitude levels, experience, and behavioural style meet your team profile. The key here is to determine the team's main strengths and ensure that the balance of member selection will be weighted to achieve the profile.

Of course, different teams within your organisation will need other profiles. A team that is required to review Risk Management measures within your organisation will require a notably different team profile than your latest product's profile for the Marketing Team.

The bottom line here is appreciating that, for your organisation to have exceptional People Management:

- You must have good people
- With the appropriately matched skill sets
- The required aptitude and behavioural profiles
- Selected to join a team that has been formed with a predetermined team profile to maximise the team's objectives

Beyond having the right people in rightly positioned roles, other strategic steps throughout the induction, onboarding, and early training phases are regular communication and demonstrations of the organisation's culture and purpose. Increasingly in highly successful organisations, employees are given access to professional coaches to assist them in mapping out what they want to achieve in their upcoming two to four years. It forms part of an organisation's culture of employee engagement, representing the levels of enthusiasm and connection that employees have with their organisation. This process measures a person's motivation to put in extra effort for their organisation and indicates how committed they are to staying there. The position of individual employee engagement is an outcome that depends on the purpose-driven actions of an organisation and the measures driven by its senior managers, supervising managers, and team leaders.

Here are some thoughts by CEOs[14] on the topic:

"Clients do not come first. Employees come first. If you take care of your employees, they will take care of the clients."
– Richard Branson, CEO and founder of Virgin Group

"To win in the marketplace you must first win in the workplace".
– Doug Conant, founder and CEO of Conant Leadership, former president and CEO of Campbell's Soup

14 Employee Engagement | Your Thought Partner - https://www.yourthoughtpartner.com/blog/10-inspiring-quotes-from-successful-ceos-to-help-you-win-at-employee-engagement

"Treat employees like they make a difference and they will."
– Jim Goodnight, CEO and co-founder of SAS Institute

"It's [employee engagement] about getting the best people, retaining them, nurturing a creative environment and helping to find a way to innovate."
– Marissa Mayer, cofounder of Lumi Labs, former CEO of Yahoo!

"Understanding your employee's perspective can go a long way towards increasing productivity and happiness."
– Kathryn Minshew, CEO and co-founder of The Muse

"Employees are a company's greatest asset – they're your competitive advantage. You want to attract and retain the best; provide them with encouragement, stimulus and make them feel that they are an integral part of the company's mission."
– Anne M. Mulcahy, former CEO and chairwoman of Xerox Corporation

"An employee's job is to give their best work every day. A manager's job is to give the employee a good reason to come back to work tomorrow."
– Liz Ryan, CEO and founder of Human Workplace

"Our mission statement about treating people with respect and dignity is not just words but a creed we live by every day. You can't expect your employees to exceed the expectations of your customers if you don't exceed the employees' expectations of management."
– Howard Schultz, former CEO and chairman of Starbucks Coffee

"There are only three measurements that tell you nearly everything you need to know about your organization's overall performance: employee engagement, customer satisfaction, and cash flow... It goes without saying that no company, small or large, can win over the long run without energized employees

who believe in the mission and understand how to achieve it."
– Jack Welch, former CEO and chairman of General Electric

People Management Summary

Beyond the established and tested quintessential needs for specific task requirements (the job), Job Specifications, Job Profiles, staff selection (recruitment), team member selection, and induction, remain the true differentiators between the average performing organisations and those recognised as being exceptional. Those components referred to in this chapter and a few other matters will become clear throughout the balance of these People Management chapters.

Regarding your people, allow me to summarise this chapter in three words; **Value, Fit,** and **Performance**. Your organisation will not become the desired entity of exceptional performance if you do not demonstrably value your people. Ensure that their fit to position, team and culture is correct and that they can meet performance targets.

6

PRACTICES MANAGEMENT

> *"People who succeed have momentum. The more they succeed, the more they want to succeed, and the more they find a way to succeed. Similarly, when someone is failing, the tendency is to get on a downward spiral that can even become a self-fulfilling prophecy."*
> **Tony Robbins**, Author

People *perform* Practices

The triple P element.

The Model advises that Practices are a People P because People *perform* Practices, and Practices *impact* Performance, which is also a People measurement. Having an organisation-wide understanding and genuine appreciation of this reinforces the position and importance of Practices within your organisation.

> ***Sideline**: As I write these opening paragraphs regarding operational elements, I can't help but wonder if you think that he repeatedly writes about the same emphasis on each operational element. If you believe that, then you are right. Still, I unapologetically again stress the importance of understanding and valuing each operational P element's relational impacts on your organisation's performance and their influence on your workplace culture.*

Consider for a moment how you operate. We all do certain things, but we often do them differently.

A perhaps trivial but practical example is: *applying toothpaste to your toothbrush; are you a top, middle, or bottom of the tube squeezer?* You might assess this individualism as creative, efficient, inefficient, or irrelevant. In the scheme of daily activities, you could judge this example as irrelevant, but is this not dependent upon its context? For instance, if you live in residence by yourself or have multiple bathrooms, how you squeeze the toothpaste tube is probably irrelevant. But if you are a member of a large household that only has one bathroom and uses one toothpaste tube, and it is the weekday early morning rush, the efficiency of your toothpaste application is essential.

Unless robots operate your organisation, these differences in human practices matter; a significant part of People Management is managing their practices. I agree with Oxford Languages (OL) definition of Practice[15], *"the actual application or use of an idea, belief, or method, as opposed to theories relating to it."*

Senior managers familiar with the P9s Practices' relational impacts state that they are the easiest to agree with due to their obvious rationale. They are also the most challenging to manage because of the infinite behavioural idiosyncrasies of team members.

Practices have the most significant influence on your organisation's culture of all the operational elements. Purpose drives culture through Protection and Policies, but ask any race car driver about their results, and they will tell you that can only be as good as the dynamics and preparation of the car they are driving. Hence, managing Practices to achieve desirable results becomes a shared responsibility.

It begins with People & Culture (which is increasingly becoming the preferred title for Human Resources) at the recruitment, selection and induction stages. The role and its fit description

15 Practice definition | Oxford Languages-https://www.lexico.com/definition/practice

(crafted before marketing the position) must include a good word picture to fit the organisation's culture well. The selection phase compels a behavioural profile match for the role and the culture.

An essential component of a new staff member's initial induction is education on your organisation's culture. Next, the upline manager's responsibility is to convincingly reinforce the importance of the cultural vibe and monitor the new member's compatibility match early in their employment term so that the person gets every opportunity to become comfortable and successful in their new role. Finally, it is up to all the other team members to encourage and support the new member while demonstrating behaviour (natural, not imposed) that exemplifies the organisation's culture.

Financial providence prefers you don't hire people if technology or robots can do the specific tasks required at an affordable cost because people have numerous additional charges. Nevertheless, when we need individuals to do particular functions unless they are purely procedural (e.g., production line), we do not want to clone them and thereby lose their creativity and intellectual contributions. So, managing their practices is not a simple matter. It requires purpose-driven strategic thought and a commitment to regular reviews.

Arguably and fortunately, the required time and resource investment in People Management can significantly impact an individual's workplace performance and subsequently return the most significant dividend to your organisation's overall performance.

R.Q. *What immediate improvements would you like to see implemented regarding the People Management of your organisation?* ***W.I.D.***

Following is the view that The Model promotes regarding the relational aspects of Practices.

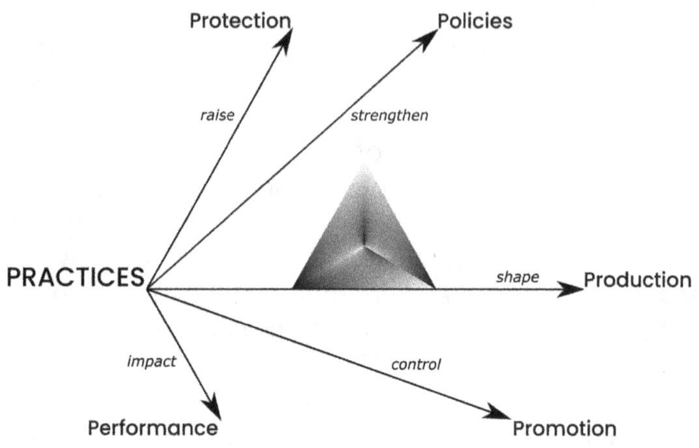

Practices *raise* Protection

> *"Organisations need to practice qualitative corporate governance rather than quantitative governance thereby ensuring it is properly run." – and "You cannot legislate good behaviour."*
> **Mervyn King** (Governor of the Bank of England from 2003 to 2013).

Of all the operational elements, Practices raise the quality of your organisation's Protection more than any of its cohort. This assertion is valid if:

- You have chosen the right people to perform the right jobs
- The jobs offered have been justified, carefully specified and correctly profiled
- Your organisation's purpose statement well articulates your enviable why factor sufficiently
- Your people daily experience evidence of your organisation's core values
- Once thoroughly explained to the new team member, your Protection Management is consistent with The Model's recommendations

Is the above list a realistic appraisal of your organisation's approach? *Yes*? Then you are a long way down the journey towards your people thinking and behaving cohesively. They will be motivated by the desire to protect the entity that provides them with a sense of worthwhileness and daily experiencing satisfaction because they are genuinely enjoying what they are doing.

Remember that the primary responsibility of your Board of Directors is to declare the organisation's objectives and expectations and provide guidance to the CEO and Executive Management Group (the owners and General Manager in a smaller business). The Board achieves this objective by insisting on adopting The P9 Management Model's paradigm and its aspirational culture, resulting in a proactive approach to Protection of all staff members.

The Board have options when they observe a concerning or potential problem with an existing governance approach. They can assume that management will fix it or that it has determined that it is not severe enough to correct. Alternatively, the Board will be proactive by referring it to The Executive Management Group and monitoring its progress.

The Board should always have a sense of ownership of the organisation's Protection. This practice is a far cry from the too-often approach of "We'll just leave it to management".

Practices *strengthen* Policies

Having arrived this far along the journey, if you accept that declaration:

- A policy's primary objective is for it to be a guiding principle that achieves the intended outcome of its creator/s
- You agree with The Model's methodology that Policies *reflect* Protection and Policies *influence* Practices,

then it is understandable for you to believe that Practices *strengthen* Policies

What will the result be?

1. You will adopt and implement The Model's methodology

2. You will continue to develop the organisational culture that you desire; together, these two will
3. Lead and motivate your staff members' thinking
4. Alter their behaviour and approach to performing required tasks
5. Move them to ensure that a policy that they and their co-workers need to comply with continues to achieve its intended outcomes
6. Ensure that the same policy's content and clarity are of the highest standard

As your staff experience the results of the above list, it will also enhance their sense of security and pride in the organisation. Your staff will experience an increased regularity of self-initiated contribution to identify issues and recommend solutions to emerging problems or performance changes. True proactivity!

Contrast this environmental experience with that of an average organisation, where the opinion and attitude of a staff member often result in them considering a policy as a burdensome, annoying and unnecessary, intrusive interruption to my day.

The difference is three words, Purpose, People and Processes! Staff members can truly experience a buy-in mentality and a desire to contribute by being and giving their best selves because they have a recognised, aspirational and respected organisational purpose of such worth. Then each phase of the process cycle delivers at a very high standard.

Practices *impact* Performance

This time-honoured relationship is arguably the easiest to accept immediately. Earlier in this chapter, you read that the Practices element covered "how we all do certain things". When I consider the Performance element, I think about **how well** a person, robot, or machine does a piece of work or activity.

So, a primary and sensible extension of that is;

- Good practices = Good performance
- Mediocre practices = Mediocre performance
- Poor practices = Poor performance

You don't necessarily need a graph or numerous examples supporting the truth that Practices *impact* Performance. You must continually tune your staff's practices to achieve the outstanding organisational performance you desire. In a 'can-do' organisation seeking sustainable excellence, a continual improvement program is essential, led from the top down, as a critical component of your workplace culture.

I expand on the above in the upcoming section on Performance Management.

As a senior manager, you must be conscious of two facts regarding your (personal) practices and performance.

1. Your team members constantly observe you
2. Your (personal) performance is conditional upon your practices, which applies to everyone

We all have practices that need improving. Most of us still have an odd bad habit that needs attention. Expecting your staff to change their unhelpful or unproductive habits while still observing your unproductive habits adds unnecessarily to the challenge of leading a continual improvement program.

R.Q. *Can you identify a personal habit that is harming your productivity? If so, and if you were managing someone with that same habit, what would you recommend they do to rectify it?* ***W.I.D.***

R.Q. *Can you identify a personal practice that harms your team's productivity? What will you do to correct it?* ***W.I.D.***

Practices *shape* Production

Shape: 'give a particular shape or form to'.

The way a person:

- Thinks
- The attitudes a person has
- Their behavioural style

will influence how they do things as much, if not more than, their experience and skillsets will impact their ability to perform a specific task.

Whether what they produce for your organisation is tangible or intangible, service-focused or product-focused, their practices matter since they shape production because of how they create something.

The goal should be to develop and implement the best practices possible. The jargon term "best practices" is often referred to in management standards. Such standards include ISO 9000 and ISO 14001. It is commonly associated with a management tool known as "benchmarking".

According to Wikipedia, *"A best practice is a method or technique that has been generally accepted as superior to any alternatives because it produces results that are superior to those achieved by other means, or because it has become a standard way of doing things, e.g., a standard way of complying with legal or ethical requirements. Best practices are used to maintain quality as an alternative to mandatory legislated standards and can be based on self-assessment or benchmarking.*[16]"

Previously the concept of Best Practices was used by operatives in law, accounting, auditing, engineering, and healthcare, but today it is used extensively in various sectors, particularly project management.

It's simply a framework for succeeding and minimising failure. Irrespective of the complexity of a task, your aim should be to make whatever you are developing or performing become better, with more efficiency and fewer problems and mistakes. So, be aware of and continually apply the best practices for what you are trying to achieve.

In developing a high performing 'can do' organisation on a journey to sustainable excellence, it is critical to routinely invest in reviewing, measuring, analysing and improving every task included in producing something. Doing this will create one of the optics of excellence.

Practices *control* Promotion

This relationship is another notable and relevant example of why The Model's operational elements' interrelational impacts need to be thoroughly understood, appreciated and applied by management. In the previous chapter on Policies Management, you read that Policies *regulate* Promotion, and, under specific conditions, Policies can control Promotion. However, the daily control of Promotion is in the Practices domain, the 'what individuals do and how they do it' realm.

Promotion is where we daily encourage the need for creativeness and the explorative nature of the human mind. Organisational or product Promotion is a product of human practices, thoughts, narratives that produce imagery, and content that answers needed information and delivers solutions. It regularly generates a desire for something previously not thought of or considered necessary.

16 Best Practice | Wikipedia - https://en.wikipedia.org/wiki/Best_practice

The direction of a specific promotion, when it forms part of an ongoing series of a particular theme or a programmed concentration of the same matter (be it an item or service, task, offering, opportunity, etc.), should be the result of:

- A predetermined evidence-based strategy, or
- An altered direction arises from a considered and measured reaction to an earlier campaign review that showed an undesired response

In addition to creating a promotion, Practices control the ongoing management of specific promotions. While there remains a need to continually monitor a promotion campaign's performance to ensure it is achieving its aim, history shows numerous examples of small incremental changes that negatively impacted the intent of a particular promotion.

Before implementing a change, a simple but good practice is to create a compulsory checklist that necessitates a person who is responsible for managing changes within the timeline of a promotion to demonstrate the following:

- Alignment to the promotion's strategic intent, or if altered, a note identifying the quantified/qualified reason for the change
- Alignment to your organisation's purpose and core values
- An updated performance target.

Completing the above checklist also maintains an audit trail, an essential practice in highly successful organisations.

Sadly, Promotion is simply the external advertising or marketing of products or services in some organisations. Overwhelmingly, this view is a misunderstanding of reality. Many internal memos contain the promotion of a specific matter. Office posters, newsletters, and emails often contain promotions.

Again quoting P.T. Barnum, who said, *"Without promotion, something terrible happens... nothing!"*

Practices Management Summary

This Practices Management chapter deserves to be the singular topic of another book, although the same is true about all other chapter topics. In particular, Practices Management is a subject matter that fascinates some managers while terrifying others.

Practices relationship directly and critically impacts each of its five cohort operational elements. Still, without further emphasis, this statement would belittle the prominence of time and energy investment required to achieve a highly successful organisation's performance.

This management area is the most challenging and potentially frustrating of all responsibilities by a reasonable distance. Concurrently, it can be the most satisfying. Get it right, and you will be the hero/heroine. It is also the most subjective of all management areas because it encompasses your uniqueness with the uniqueness of every team member.

Your role is to make the differences between individual practices and preferences mesh rather than clash. This skill is foundational in creating synergy and leveraging gains. Your commitment to mastering the "mesh rather than clash" setting is mandatory in an organisation seeking sustainable excellence. Beyond your willingness to commit to this, your will need to develop or improve particular personal skillsets.

Understanding and valuing the principles and detailed ideology structure of The Model is a vital step on the ladder to organisational success. Still, it will also require you to know what levers are available to use in managing Practices. Once you see what those levers are, you will need to become experienced in knowing how, when, why and how far to adjust each lever. Right there is another differentiator between the average manager and the exceptional manager!

7

PERFORMANCE MANAGEMENT

> *"Management is, in the end, the most creative of all the arts—for its medium is human talent itself."*
> **Robert S. McNamara**, former US Secretary of Defence

Of all the possible and variable influence factors, The Model advocates that your people will predominantly determine your organisation's performance.

It is always good to dig deeper into several highly successful organisations, to observe and analyse how they execute Performance Management.

Performance Management is no longer just a performance appraisal or a disciplinary process but instead aims to improve organisation-wide functionality by creating balanced teams and assisting individual performances.

Affective performance management measures the progress occurring towards accomplishing the organisation's objectives. Additionally, having managers experienced in understanding and valuing the relational impacts between Performance and its five (operational) cohort elements develops and sustains a holistic style of performance management that maximises positive results. This synergetic process is The P9 Management Model's approach.

> *"Insanity is doing the same thing, over and over again, but expecting different results."*
> **Albert Einstein**

Far too many organisations have a habit of repeating poor to mediocre performance. They repeatedly make identical mistakes because management fails to identify problematic behaviour effectively. It is not analysed and recorded (journalized). Managers move on, staff leave, or transfer to other departments, resulting in lost intellectual property. Not amending counter-productive Practices results in workplace cultures not changing!

The Model inspires senior managers to avoid such experiences by developing and maintaining methods that monitor, record, analyse and promptly amend performance contributing components when necessary.

Essentially, organisational performance begins with the individual.

Position Design: Develop strategically considered and well-written specifications for a potential staff member's role (Job Descriptions). This description is an excellent opportunity to introduce additional factors beyond the tasks, essential experience, and minimum required qualifications. It can (and usually should) include a Job Profile for the role (see more detail in the People Management chapter) and, where appropriate, the role's contribution and fit to the team it operates in.

Staff Selection: Beyond the well-established staff selection traditions for meeting (selected) criteria, you should lift the bar to entry when selecting a staff member. Many might meet your chosen standards, but will they be the right fit?

Ask yourself, is the person applying for the role capable of and naturally suited to contributing to your organisation's purpose? Will they work comfortably with your workplace culture? Ideally, your organisation (already has or) should develop a Purpose

Statement with elements similar to that referred to in the Purpose Management chapter. Such *a purpose will incorporate ideals of advancement and deliver meaning that often inspires the collective, committed to such standards, to persist and push through otherwise impenetrable obstacles.*

Scenario: Applicant 1 meets or exceeds the traditional criteria but will struggle to honestly buy into your organisation's purpose and adapt to its culture. Applicant 2 could perform the role but will require further investment to meet your standards; however, they would be an excellent 'values and culture' fit for your organisation.

Recommendation: I would strongly recommend you consider selecting the second candidate.

Induction and Onboarding present a potentially significant gain. Recent surveys show that most organisations continually improve new staff induction processes. However, there are still far too few that maximise this once-off opportunity to introduce a new staff member to your organisation's purpose, core values and workplace culture in such a way as to infuse excitement, agreement and commitment.

> ***Quick TIP:*** Create a short, well-crafted clip (generic) of you (as the CEO) welcoming a new team member in which you express your commitment to the organisation's core values and workplace culture. Then, 48 hours later, follow it up with a personalised email (with pertinent content info prepared by your People & Culture staff) containing specific details about the individual's suitability for their new role. This email demonstrates your endorsement of their selection as a new team member of an exceptional organisation. Further, it confirms their confidence in making the right choice to apply for the role.

The respect and value you genuinely possess and demonstrate towards every staff member, combined with the expressed organisation's investment in individuals, beyond wages and oncosts, will pay very healthy returns to bottom-line results, sustainable performance and reputation.

Exceptional organisations develop exceptional workplace cultures! Some existing commonalities include (in alphabetical, not a priority, order):

- Care Beyond Their Job Role
- Career Pathways
- Education
- Employee Mentoring
- Evaluations & Reviews
- Flexibility
- Recognition
- Reward
- Team Building
- Work/life Balance considerations

Care Beyond Their Job Role: Beyond a mere acknowledgment of a team member's birthday, a brief celebratory email or SMS from one or more of your Executive Management Team members, and a small gift (which you may offer them as a choice from a small selection of options; such as various store gift cards, or an E-book voucher) can be an affordable way of expressive care. It is not the gift's value that they focus on long term, as much as their sense of being valued. The messages and gifts should never become a promoted practice or policy, thus undermining their purpose.

EOTF (End Of Trip Facilities) is another (growingly popular) way of demonstratively valuing your staff. For those who, rather than driving or taking public transport to attend their workplace, cycle, scoot, skate, jog, or walk, or who like to exercise before or after work or during their lunch break, EOTF are places or rooms within a business or office building designed to support such people.

EOTF usually include:

- Locker facilities

- Secure bicycle/scooter parking or storage
- Showers and change rooms

Some organisations even offer extra self-usage features such as ironing facilities, clothes steamers, hairdryers, and styling tools to help employees freshen up and prepare for their workday. Some exceptional organisations include bike repair stations for any unforeseen accidents on the way to work. EOTF are proving to have additional benefits, including:

- An overall healthier workforce
- Enhanced corporate image
- Increased productivity
- Increased staff wellbeing
- Reduced demand for car parking

Numerous surveys are sustaining the argument for EOTF, including one by the City of Sydney[17].

Career Pathways: Beyond the new team member's starting position, clear and attractive advanced career options are increasingly crucial for skilled workers when choosing employment offerings. Numerous examples exist of individuals that give up an initially higher wage package to go with an organisation that offers other benefits, including specified aspirational pathways. These expectations are increasingly common in organisations experiencing rapid and sustainable growth, but utilising some *'thinking out of the box'* style management, can still be realistic in more mainstream entities.

Education: There are numerous ways to satisfy a person's desire for ongoing education, including:

- Well-produced internal development training sessions

17 End Of Trip Facilities survey | City of Sydney - https://www.cityofsydney.nsw.gov.au/surveys-case-studies-reports/active-transport-survey-2021

- Industry association provided training courses
- Government and private colleges which provide certificate and diploma courses
- Using online private service providers of recognised certificate and diploma courses
- Universities

Funding attendance and study time arrangements can vary from policy-driven to individual negotiation. For instance, funding options include:

- Fully funded by the employer (for higher levels of education, there may need to be a contractual year of employee ***retainment*** agreement, with an exit option that allows the employee to repay costs to date partially [seek legal opinion]). Fully funded education may occur discretionally as a reward for exceptional performance
- Partially funded by the employer
- Salary sacrificed
- Partially funded by the employer and salary sacrificed

Employee Mentoring: Where appropriate, this can form part of an employee's professional development plan. Mentoring or coaching can be as structured or straightforward as required and desired.

For example, you can have two co-workers with different experience levels engaged in an informal mentorship. This method is an excellent way to support productive workplace relationships and increase one employee's skill and knowledge development while developing the other employee's training skills.

Alternately, it can be a structured mentoring program that might include 30 minutes a month with an Executive Management Team member for a team member identified as a future executive candidate.

Evaluations & Reviews: Many organisations still apply traditionally thinking to their staff evaluations or reviews. Such organisations heavily weigh their assessments towards performance. By doing so, they miss an excellent opportunity to access further intellectual property and to assess the overall well-being of the team member, including their:

- The present level of role and KPI's achievement (including comparisons to previously set personal goals),
- Continuing fit to their current team or their ongoing fit to your organisation
- Sense of mental health
- Changing aspirations
- Work/life balance
- Assessment of:
  - Their upline manager
  - Their team
  - You (as CEO)
  - Your organisation

Flexibility: Workplace flexibility has been a hot topic for over a decade, yet no one could have predicted how the COVID19 pandemic would affect workplace operations. Organisations left without an alternative were forced to adapt.

As a result, a new mindset has emerged, and along with it is a new term 'hybrid working'. For the first time, many organisations have considered and implemented numerous workplace and operational changes, including working hours, working days, working mode, location, and job and role sharing. In productivity and profitability measures, such implementation's success varies depending on the organisation. Increasingly, some employers are experiencing operating cost reductions. One identified potentially harmful hybrid working matter for employees is a lack of purpose, which will require attention from your Executive Management Team (see the report prepared by Wharton[18]).

The future of hybrid working is not set in concrete. My opinion is that it will evolve and offer both employees and employers still to be discovered benefits. I believe the future will also present opportunities for further development in workplace flexibility thinking and increased collaboration between senior management and operational staff.

Recognition: Is recognising an individual not just the beginning of basic respect? As a component of Esteem, Recognition is the 2nd highest level on Maslow's hierarchy of human needs. Recognition of every team member as an individual should be a management prerequisite. I recommend it become a priority inclusion in your organisation's Core Values Statement.

Recognition of the individual is a foundational cornerstone in performance management, and depending on your mindset and focus, it is a relatively low fruit offering. It is certainly not burdensome. It starts by simply remembering someone's name and some of their details, including their current role in your organisation.

Some additional recognitions might include:

- The acknowledgement of their birthday

---

18 Hybrid Working | Wharton - http://d1c25a6gwz7q5e.cloudfront.net/reports/2020-11-09-workplace-whitepaper-FINAL.pdf

- A recognition of their anniversary with your organisation
- A complimentary nickname (of course, only with the voluntary consent of the team member and ceased to be used if such consent is ever retracted)

Many entities demonstrate recognition in awards, such as Team Member of the Month or Culture Advocate. Of course, this form of reward focuses on the individual and is limited to one person. The additional option of awarding the 'Role of the Month' can bring value recognition to many individuals and remind your entire staff of the Role's contribution and value to the organisation.

Reward: Performance Management has many levers available, including Rewards and Incentives, which can be beneficial. However, there is a distinct difference in timing and purpose. Incentives are employee benefits offered as motivation to improve their productivity or behaviour. It is a pre-performance offering or promise. A reward (or an award) is a post-event item given for past contributions, not limited to performance nor necessarily public recognition. There are varying rewards categories, e.g. personal, group, and organisation-wide.

Examples of personal rewards include:

- A catered lunch
- A gift to the charity of their choice
- A feature in the organisation's newsletter
- A music subscription
- A remote workday
- Bike/scooter share membership
- Books & ebooks
- Cash
- Concert tickets

- Corporate branded clothing & items
- Fitness class
- Gift cards
- Lunch with an executive
- Paid time off

For more Reward examples, just search examples of workplace rewards.

Whatever the reward, ensure its presentation demonstrates the team member's value and contribution.

Team Building: Managing teams is another significant opportunity to increase organisational performance and show respect and value to each team member. You have already read numerous words regarding an individual's job and team fit in this and previous chapters. So, presuming you already have the right people in the right jobs and join the right teams, you must ensure that the organisation gets the best possible outcomes from those teams.

A good start is to appoint the most suitable team leader and provide them with all the appropriate resources, including top-rated task management tools and software that enables the desired collaboration, planning, task management, and tracking progress. As a minimum, the team leader needs to:

- Be a clear, effective communicator
- Be a decision-maker
- Be a problem solver
- Be open and approachable
- Be organised
- Have or be developing a high level of emotional intelligence

- Be totally cognitive and entirely in agreement with your organisation's purpose statement and core values

When forming a new team to perform one-off specific tasks, the initial meeting with the selected team leader needs to layout, as a minimum, the following:

- The team's objectives
- The timeline for a final result
- Scheduled progress updates and the communication mode/s between the team leader and yourself,
- The budget
- The initial resources
- The criteria for team member selection

An essential factor in building a successful team is having each selected team member value the team's objectives and a desire to contribute to the team.

Managing a team in the above-described style has multiple benefits, including retaining a reputation for best practices, maintaining an achievement culture, and sustaining the desired goal of having all team members again experience a sense of the organisation's appreciation and value of their staff.

Work/life Balance considerations: Perhaps the best method of demonstrating your organisation's respect for and value of each staff member is to show a genuine concern for their work/life balance. Everyone has a life outside of the workplace, and for each of us, that life is different. We have differing family makeups, responsibilities, priorities, pursuits, activities, hobbies, ambitions, goals, and dreams.

In this chapter (and the previous chapter), you have already read numerous suggestions of how you can demonstrate appropriate respect, recognition and reward for the contribution of an individual staff member. I want to make a critical point now. Your responsibility is to have every individual's upline manager and a team member of your People and Culture Team make it their responsibility to know sufficient detail about every staff member. Then, they need to consider and determine if there are additional ways your organisation could improve the work-life balance of that individual.

I began this chapter by stating, *"Of all the possible and variable influence factors, The Model advocates that your people will predominantly determine your organisation's performance."* If implemented, the contents of this opening section on Performance Management will be considerable. It will be a massive step towards moving your organisation's performance from its current level to being among those recognised as exceptional.

R.Q. *In your opinion, how do the matters raised in this section align with the reality of your organisation?* ***W.I.D.***

People *determine* Performance

You are becoming increasingly familiar with The Model's core elements of Purpose, People, and Processes. You know that the cohort elements of People are Practices and Performance. I want to remind you that the impacting relationship People has on Performance is determination, hence the declaration that People *determine* Performance.

I'm a long-time fan of Formula 1 motor racing (F1), for it has long been the pinnacle of automotive progress and at the forefront of human endeavour.

One of my heroes was Sir John Arthur Brabham (1926-2014), AO OBE. He was an Australian racing driver who was Formula One World Champion in 1959, 1960, and 1966. He was a founder of the Brabham racing team and race car constructor that bore his name.

"Sir Jack Brabham[19] also won the automobile constructors' championship twice (1966 and 1967). Brabham was a Royal Australian Air Force flight mechanic and ran a small engineering workshop before racing midget cars in 1948. His successes with Midgets in Australian and New Zealand road racing events led to his going to Britain to further his racing career. He became part of the Cooper Car Company's racing team, building and racing cars.

He contributed to the design of the mid-engine cars that Cooper introduced to Formula One and the Indianapolis 500 and won the Formula One world championship in 1959 and 1960. In 1962 he established his own Brabham marque with fellow Australian Ron Tauranac, which in the 1960s became the largest manufacturer of customer racing cars in the world. In the 1966 Formula One season **Brabham became the first – and still, the only – man to win the Formula One world championship driving one of his own cars**. He was the last surviving World Champion of the 1950s."

There are critical factors in winning an F1 race.

- The selection of a driver
- The design and construction of a race car
- The selection and performance of the Team Manager
- The choice of the pit team
- The time it takes to perform a mid-race pit stop

Beyond those, many other matters and items also influence a win.

When Brabham won his first championship **in 1959, it took approximately 30 seconds** to complete a pit stop. **Today it takes less than 2 seconds** to jack off the ground the front and rear of the car, change all four tyres, adjust front and rear stabiliser bars, perform front wing adjustment, and clean the driver's helmet visor.

---

19 Sir Jack Brabham | Wikipedia - https://en.wikipedia.org/wiki/Jack_Brabham

Today, there are more pit crew members, and significant technological advances have occurred. There has also been a focus on the pit crew psychology required, physical fitness and fit for team skills, data analysis, communication methods, team harmony, and perpetual practising to improve performance.

Imagine what the world would look like if every organisation took the same approach to such outrageously ambitious progress in operational performance and organisational outcomes.

Reality check: If you have worked through every previous chapter of this book and considered and answered the **Q** questions, you are not the average manager or leader. Neither will your organisation remain average. It will not tolerate mediocrity. Even if, in future maintenance seasons, static performance is necessary, it will suffer such periods with much frustration. It aims for the highest altitude within its sector and then some.

You agree that People *determine* Performance (by now, that should be a given) and that you now have a considerable understanding of People Management within The Model's context. In that case, you should be thorough in gaining your knowledge of the interrelational impacts of Performance on its cohort operational elements.

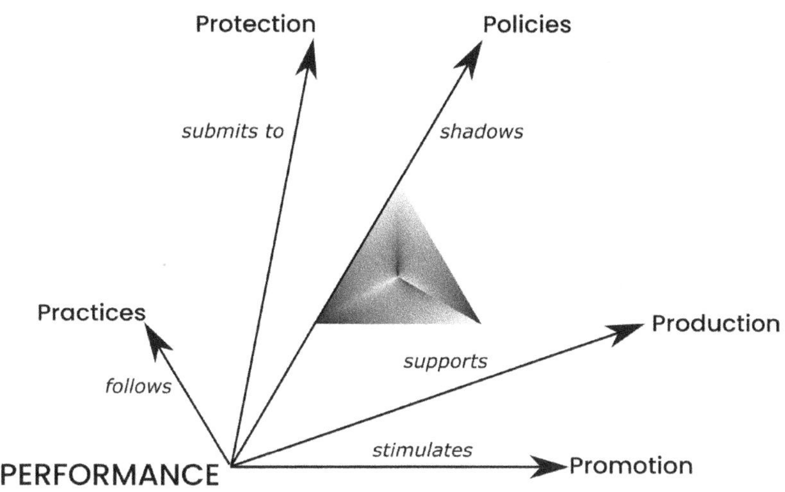

Performance *submits to* Protection

Now is another opportune moment to restate a comment from The P9 Management Model (explanation) chapter where I stated that "The P9 Management Model is the **Think Big** view of your organisation. It is more than just a general understanding of the macro view". It goes beyond thinking of your organisation as a group of departments doing various activities by introducing the concept of critical areas of management responsibility.

In many organisations, performance is considered by only measuring specific KPIs, such as the rate of total revenue increase, net profit and an improved Balance Sheet (Statement of Position). However, the paradigm focus behind The P9 Management Model is **The Pursuit Of Excellence Within Your Organisation.** It is a view of Organisational Success that differs from the norm. It includes the established KPIs and adds some KEIs (Key Excellence Indicators), including:

- Corporate Citizenship
- Customer/Client Satisfaction Levels
- Employee's Satisfaction Levels

- Organisation Culture Outcomes
- Processes' Improvement Program status
- Results to purpose Fitness

Any competent CEO can improve the profitability of a corporation. More competent CEOs can enhance their corporation's Balance Sheet. But achieving exceptional performance and sustainable excellence requires the combination of an inspiring CEO, an outstanding Executive Management Team and a purpose-focused workforce. The collective performance of your people will determine your organisation's overall performance.

Protection *enhances* Performance, and Performance *submits to* Protection. Exceptional organisations develop and continually improve their Protection Management, not just as a traditional contingent insurance program but as a vehicle that positively influences their organisation's performance.

In an organisation that adopts The Model, you will observe that Performance gains from Protection, thus implementing a workplace culture where Performance *submits to* Protection is not just possible, or even probable, but inevitable. Organisation-wide respect for the purpose and the continuing positive outcomes of Protection Management makes this a reality.

Performance *shadows* Policies

Policies *reflect* Protection, and Protection *enhances* Policies. Within the first core element, Purpose, The Model has a natural progression pathway from Protection to Policies, and Policies *reflect* Protection.

The immediately above section focused on the relationship between Performance and Protection, being one of submission, because of the highly valued importance of Protection. Policies are the vehicle that Protection uses to guide and control governance.

In a highly successful organisation, from an individual's induction through every stage of their tenure, they are encouraged to strive to understand their employer's Protection Management element and the Policy Management element. Such knowledge and appreciation of these areas of responsibility greatly assist each staff member in reflecting on their performance and contribution to the organisation.

Two foundational components of Performance are opinion and attitude because opinions form the attitudes we hold. A lack of knowledge and misunderstandings of your organisation's policies' detail and value will result in unintended and undesirable workplace attitudes. The alternate and opposite outcome occurs when there is a deliberately consistent interface between staff and your organisation's Purpose's operational elements of Protection and Policies.

When there is a high opinion of the value of your organisation's policies, your staff will form positive attitudes and do everything they can to increase their performance. You will find that a team member, transformed from a negative to a positive attitude, will follow your organisation's policies more diligently. The same staff member will become keen to contribute to policy promotion and improvement.

Performance *follows* Practices

Practices *impact* Performance, and Performance *follows* Practices. Acknowledging those two statements is a prerequisite step towards competently managing Performance. Performance is a practical measurement of Practices; the better practices, the better the performance outcomes will be.

Achieving a sub-two seconds mid-race pit stop in Formula 1 has taken sixty years of pit crew training and numerous technological advancements. The critical practice areas of each crew member include:

- Psychological: A regular assessment of the overall health of their headspace, maintaining a clear focus, isolating distractions, having powerful self-confidence, continually possessing a situational awareness approach, and retaining a strong sense of success

- Physical fitness: Maintaining a physical capacity to do the task without becoming tired or task deteriorating.
- Fit for team skills: Gaining and maintaining all the skills (people and practical) necessary to retain their place on the team
- Data analysis: Being familiar with the presented information and knowing how to maximise results.
- Communication methods: Participating, contributing clearly, critically listening, observing body language, and responding appropriately
- Team harmony: Being an enthusiastic contributor to peace by actions, words, and body language
- Perpetual repetitive performance routines: Maximising every occasion to improve

Notice how each of the above practice areas applies to the performance of individuals performing various tasks in organisations representing every sector, including your organisation.

There are two key individuals in a Formula 1 team: the Driver and the Team Manager, always selected based on their historical performance-based experiences. They both receive high salaries. The team owners and sponsors rightfully highly value them. Yet once the driver correctly positions the race car for a pit stop, the sub-two seconds outcome relies only on the twenty pit crew members' performances. The pit crew cannot solely win the race event for the race team, but they can certainly lose it.

The practices of every individual in your organisation are essential in achieving your desired workplace culture and performance targets. Invest in knowing what their practices contribute, and where necessary, ensure that a counterproductive practice is appropriately modified.

Performance *supports* Production

While Practices (the way one does things) *shape* Production, our mental approach to a task potentially supports (enhances and strengthens) the product of that task. Maintaining a can-do attitude motivates the initiation of a job and increases the desire to analyse and continually improve each procedural step.

Driven by the performance improvement paradigm, each stage's procedural order requires evaluation to ensure efficiency and quality optimisation when the end product requires multiple steps.

Performance Management is a crucial prerequisite of Production Management. Be it a tangible product or a service, the better the performance levels of your people, will produce the following:

- Better quality of tools/equipment for production
- Faster construction times
- More focused improvements to:
  - Design
  - Procedures
  - User-friendliness (in construction)
  - Improved component compatibility
  - Finished product performance
  - Customer/client satisfaction and loyalty
- Improvement to your overall organisation's performance by improving:
  - Efficiency
  - Levels of job satisfaction
  - Harmony in the workspace and overall workplace
  - Profitability
  - Corporate reputation

Performance *stimulates* Promotion

You can offer your client or customer an improved product or service by achieving the above. Whenever you improve your product or service, your promotion team is inspired to think of new ways to promote the enhanced product/service.

The above improvement often introduces opportunities for considering a revamped promotional campaign and developing parallel or additional promotional themes to attract different categories of clients/customers.

You will be surprised by your promotion team's creativity and quality results once you experience organisation-wide confidence in one of your products or services. Such confidence increases when that product/service has benefited from higher individual and group (team) performance levels by multiple people or teams contributing. Even in some exceptional organisations, that does not always occur. Nevertheless, it should always be desired.

On such occasions, the performance of individuals created the improved product, but the product's performance stimulates the promotion team. Then you will observe that the stimulated promotion team's performance further encourages their work; thus, you have the power of synergy before your eyes.

This same matter of performance improvement applies to items that need promotion internally. However, there is an automatic unequal gain that has already occurred. Where an external promotion requires a level of marketplace education, internal promotion benefits from the existence of a class of confidence and enthusiasm by all those who contributed to whatever needs promoting (an altered organisation direction, a takeover or merger, policies, a new or modified product or service, etc.).

Another gain occurs when those team members who take pride in their contribution to the production of an item that requires promotion react negatively to the form or style of that product's marketing. Not by the traditional behaviour of whinging or criticising, but by effectively engaging with the promotional team to achieve an improved outcome. Occasionally, an inappropriate marketing theme results when those responsible for creating a promotional campaign:

- have been underinformed
- misinformed, or
- misunderstood one or more peculiarities of the new or altered item, product or service

Performance Management Summary

The contents of this chapter do not adequately cover the raft of areas involved in Performance Management. It intends to deal with the basics, the prerequisite in assisting you to become an exceptional senior manager and better understand how Performance impacts its cohort operational elements.

Of all the tasks that you, as the CEO, or Senior Manager of a particular department, are responsible for, Performance Management is where you will invest most of your time.

I am confident that you (already did or do now) appreciate the various required skillsets essential to excel in Performance Management. Subsequently, it begins with your performance, which starts with your opinions and attitudes. It is rare in life that an adult will declare that their views and perspectives have never changed. That which you were so sure of, and articulated so enthusiastically just a decade or a little more ago, is no longer your view.

What changed? How did you get it wrong? What has it taught you? Three rhetorical questions.

What changed was simply that time enabled you to experience different situations or circumstances that challenged and ultimately altered your opinion and attitude on that matter. What happened was that you grew intellectually and in wisdom. That is life, particularly as a CEO or a senior manager.

You did not necessarily get it wrong. You formed views and perspectives that you believed were correct based on your observations and experiences up until that season in life. You then discovered that it required a different approach under a separate and diverse set of circumstances in another situation, and consequently, you navigated yourself to developing a new view.

It taught you, as it teaches all of us, that we must remain humble and be willing to adapt to change. This adaptability is indeed the regular experience of exceptional CEOs.

Performance is the gain changer!

Almost any manager can extrude more productivity from their employees by imposing external pressure. But that style of management only succeeds in one of two outcomes. It only produces short-term gains or creates a culture of frustration and negativity.

The P9 Management Model styled manager strategically develops an environment that encourages, incentivises and rewards an internal, intrinsic desire within each team member to want to go the extra mile. The resulting productivity and quality gains far outweigh the financial cost of the desired workplace culture, an enviable, can-do-better, harmonious and cohesive environment.

I opened this chapter by stating, *"The P9 Management Model advocates that your people will predominantly determine your organisation's performance."* You, as CEO, may well be the chosen organisation's driver. Still, you will never win a race without a high-performance pit crew. You could even cause your organisation to drop into a lower performance class category (think stock market indexes). Alternatively, you could drive your team to win the next championship.

Under your command, you are responsible for providing yourself and every individual with the resources, encouragement, support, and reward for continually operating at the highest possible performance levels.

8

PROCESSES MANAGEMENT

> "Without continual growth and progress, such words as improvement, achievement, and success have no meaning."
> **Benjamin Franklin**, 6th President of Pennsylvania

Design & Refine!

The Model recognises Processes as the final of its three core elements.

Remember my first mantra, "A worthy & defined **Purpose** delivered by valued **People** utilising highly developed **Processes** = organisational success leading to sustainable excellence!" Another business mantra of mine is "*The P9 Management Model's success essentially relies upon the quality of the daily decisions of you and your management team.*" You can read more on that mantra in the later chapter, *The P9 Decision Making Matrix.*

Purpose inspires, People respond, and Processes deliver! In the earlier Practices Management chapter, I focused on the activities of human beings, *what they do and how they do it.*

In this chapter, the focus is broader. It recognises that *a process* is different to *a practice*. Nevertheless, to ensure that we are singing from the same song sheet, my long-held simple definition of a process is **a sequence of actions or steps undertaken to achieve a particular outcome**. Hence, in an era of fast-moving progression and reliance on automation, robotics and artificial intelligence advancements, we accept that specific processes do not always rely upon direct human involvement.

Naturally and undeniably, there is a measure of collaboration between Practices Management and Processes Management.

You may wonder why I speak of Processes Management rather than Process Management (a common term in the business world). At first glance, it may seem pedantic, but it is part of the "Think Big" paradigm. Using the term Processes rather than Process enables a broader, more inclusive list of descriptive actions. Remember reading that ***"The P9 Management Model is the Think Big view of your organisation****. It does not represent specific divisions or departments but critical areas of management responsibility. Indeed, it is likely that every division or department will engage with and utilise each 'P' element. It is a more sophisticated and philosophical approach to management that empowers your quest for knowledge and wisdom and improves your ability to deal with obstacles."*

Terminologies, acronyms, and jargon! While every sector has them, Management Consulting is at the forefront of this postmodernist phenomenon. The fields of Process Improvement and Business Process Management are no exceptions. Some terms you may be familiar with include 5S technique, Cause and Effect Analysis, DMAIC, Kaizen, Kanban, PDCA, Process Mapping, SIPOC Analysis, Six Sigma, Total Quality Management, and Value Stream Mapping.

The Management Consulting sector promotes that each technique is uniquely valued because it accommodates a different need, such as changing the company's culture, lean process improvement techniques, or mapping out process workflows.

R.Q. *What has been your 'Processes' journey to date?* ***W.I.D.***

R.Q. *What is your understanding and view of managing the processes within your organisation?* ***W.I.D.***

> William Edwards Deming - ***"It is not enough to do your best; you must know what to do, and then do your best."***

Deming (1900-1993) was an American engineer, statistician, professor, author, lecturer, and management consultant. He was also a remarkable professional in Process Improvement, regularly credited with helping Japan rebuild itself following World War II. The U.S. Department of the Census and the Bureau of Labor Statistics continues to use his work on Sampling Techniques.

My initial understanding of Process Improvement derived from studying Deming's books, papers and illustrations. His above statement brilliantly defines Processes Management. Wanting *to do your best* is a great start, but not knowing the what, with who, when, where, why, and how of 'doing it' will rarely produce a successful result.

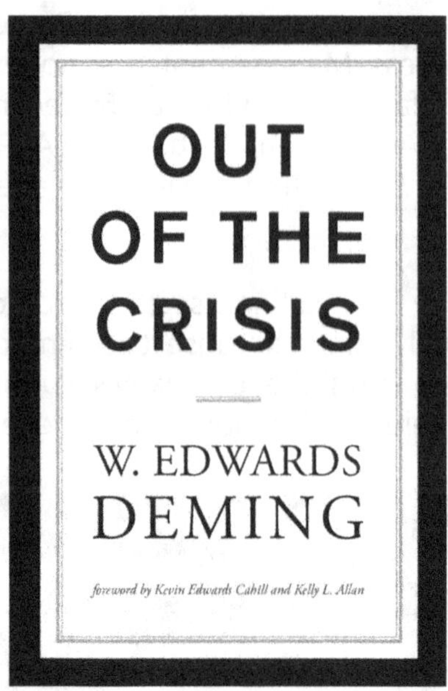

In his book *Out Of The Crisis*[20], he detailed what he described as the system of transformation based on 14 Points that he noted later in his book with sufficient explanations. Those points are:

1. *Create constancy of purpose toward improvement of product and service, with the aim to become competitive and to stay in business, and to provide jobs.*
2. *Adopt the new philosophy. We are in a new economic age. Western management must awaken to the challenge, must learn their responsibilities, and take on leadership for change.*
3. *Cease* dependence *on inspection to achieve quality. Eliminate the need for inspection on a mass basis by building quality into the product in the first place.*
4. *End the practice of awarding business on the basis of price tag. Instead, minimize total cost. Move toward a single supplier for any one item, on a long-term relationship of loyalty and trust.*

20 Process Improvement | Deming, W. Edwards. foreword by Kevin Edwards Cahill and Kelly L. Allan., Out Of The Crisis © 2018 Massachusetts Institute of Technology, by permission of The MIT Press.

5. *Improve constantly and forever the system of production and service, to improve quality and productivity, and thus constantly decrease costs.*

6. *Institute training on the job.*

7. *Institute leadership. The aim of supervision should be to help people and machines and gadgets to do a better job. Supervision of management is in need of overhaul, as well as supervision of production workers.*

8. *Drive out fear, so that everyone may work effectively for the company.*

9. *Break down barriers between departments. people in research, design, sales, and production must work as a team, to foresee problems of production and in use that may be encountered with the product or service.*

10. *Eliminate slogans, exhortations, and targets for the workforce asking for zero defects and new levels of productivity. Such exhortations only create adversarial relationships, as the bulk of the causes of low quality and low productivity belong to the system and thus lie beyond the power of the workforce.*

11a. *Eliminate work standards (quotas) on the factory floor. Substitute leadership.*

11b. *Eliminate management by objective. Eliminate management by numbers, and numerical goals. Substitute leadership.*

12a. *Remove barriers that rob the hourly worker of his right to pride of workmanship. The responsibility of supervisors must be changed from sheer numbers to quality.*

12b. *Remove barriers that rob people in management and in engineering of their right to pride of workmanship. This means, inter alia, abolishment of the annual or merit rating and of management by objective.*

13. *Institute a vigorous program of education and self-improvement.*

14. *Put everybody in the company to work to accomplish the transformation. The transformation is everybody's job.*

In a growing number of organisations, you could argue that a selection of those points is now quite common.

Already mentioned above is the area of Business Process Management. It is now another specialised area that has gained popularity. Its practitioners use various methods to identify, analyse, measure, model, improve, optimise, and automate business processes. As a leading entity in Business Process Management, Gartner[21] defines business process management as: *"the discipline of managing processes (rather than tasks) as the means for improving business performance outcomes and operational agility. Processes span organizational boundaries, linking together people, information flows, systems, and other assets to create and deliver value to customers and constituents."*

Process Improvement and Business Process Management are contemporary management consultants' most concentrated offerings. There is no area of management that they do not cover, as every task benefits from continual analysis and improvement. There exists a vast array of material on the internet regarding Process Improvement and Business Process Management. Just perform a browser search on it and prepare to be swamped with information.

Subject to your experience level in senior management, you will probably be familiar with some or even many of their promoted models and frameworks, similar to various tools used in other daily senior management tasks. Alternately, you may just be beginning to educate yourself in a relevant process area within your organisation that requires your attention. Based on either scenario, you will understand why I do not intend to comprehensively explain the multitude of detailed content involved in Process Improvement and Business Process Management.

Also, as I stated in the Preface, *"One book does not make us an expert; this only happens when one has a significant measure of both knowledge and experience."*

21 Business Process Management | Gartner - https://www.gartner.com/en

A crucial point to understand about being an exceptional CEO; you no longer need to be the expert (of your previous area of specialisation). Of course, you have a history of becoming educated, qualified and experienced in a specialised area. You have spent years on further professional development and honing your skillsets, but now you have reached (or are aiming for) the CEO role. Now you seek (and are responsible) to employ the best-fit, highest qualified and most suitable experts available in each critical role within your Executive Management Team.

The following quote from a INC.com[22] page summarises it well: *"Smart leaders hire people who are way smarter than themselves. But how do they maintain the respect of their employees? Most leaders rose through the ranks because they were experts in a particular field. But once you're at the top, your expertise in a specific field is less relevant. You need to lead the team, and you can't get hung up on not being the best-informed person in the room.*

Wanda Wallace, president and CEO of coaching and consulting firm Leadership Forum, and David Creelman, CEO of human capital management firm Creelman Research, write in Harvard Business Review[23] about how leaders deal with not being an expert anymore.

---

22 Smart Leadfers | INC.com - https://www.inc.com/will-yakowicz/how-to-lead-when-youre-the-dumbest-team-member.html

23 CEO expertise | Harvard Business Review - https://hbr.org/2015/06/leading-people-when-they-know-more-than-you-do

"Leaders who come up from an expertise track almost always derail here, because they react to the challenge by relying on their core strengths: high intelligence and the capacity for hard work," Wallace and Creelman write. The duo say you should refrain from trying to be an expert when you reach this level. You have more important things to do, and your team has all the expertise you need."

You don't have to be a sector leader in Process Improvement and Business Process Management. Your role is to lead your key people in such a manner as to extract the best from them. You or your predecessor employed them as experts. Most non-manufacturing organisations have hundreds of tasks that no one individual manager could ever be across in a detailed manner. Manufacturing organisations have thousands. You must retain a macro approach but with a P9 Think Big mindset.

Reality Check. The above requires you to have healthy self-esteem (based on a realistically balanced assessment, not an overly heightened ego), be confident in your competencies and capacities, and possess a determination to achieve your goals.

The P9 Management Model styled manager must focus on optimising the three core and six operational elements to provide the desired organisation success. They must lead their Executive Management Team in a manner that empowers them, the experts, to individually deliver highly refined processes necessary to achieve the targets and objectives.

Again, I stress that each core element within The Model is exclusively unique and highly valuable. Their position, intent, sophistication, and essential contribution are compelling and irresistible to the CEO committed to conquering mediocrity and delivering sustainable excellence.

Alignment

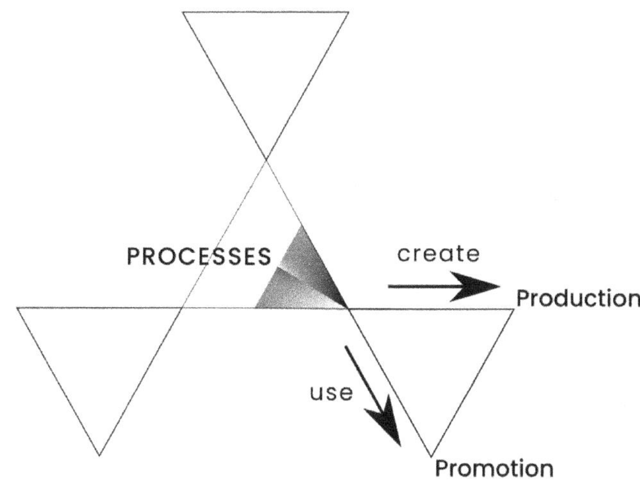

The balance of this chapter briefly focuses on the relational impacts of Processes on its two cohort operation elements, Production and Promotion. It then considers their interrelational implications with their respective cohort operational elements.

Processes Management is when the theory, planning, preliminary work, prototypes, etc., go into action.

People utilise (conceptualise, plan, design, develop, prototype, test, analyse, refine and repeatedly reassess with the aim of improvement) these highly developed **processes**, whether performed by humans or automated.

Production: Your organisation produces something, be it a tangible product or a service. Creating it necessitates specific processes, confirming that Processes *create* Production because the more advanced and effective the techniques are, the better the product.

Promotion: Once you have any beneficial product (targeting internal or external users), it requires promotion. The team responsible for promotion will need direction. The determined direction will itself be a product of processes (identifying intended usage, practical benefits, anticipated time to market, etc.). Hence, The Model advocates that Processes *deploy* Promotion.

Processes Management Summary

Of the three core elements, Processes Management is the one that many CEOs feel most comfortable with due to their career involvement to date. Still, this area of responsibility is so vast that few can claim extensive expertise. There are at least two potential books with a P9 focus worthy of existence on the above contents of Processes Management. However, for the moment, you will already know that there exist volumes of relevant material in the marketplace. I recommend that you seek an author whose expository discourse covers a particularly pertinent topic of your needs.

Earlier in this chapter, you read, *"There is a crucial point to understand about being an exceptional CEO; you no longer need to be an expert."* Whatever has been your pathway to the CEO's office confirms that you cannot be an expert in all P9 Elements, nor is that expected of you. You have employed experts to perform exceptionally in their particular field. Your role is to set out the directions, lead, monitor, and make critical decisions. Leave the necessary micromanagement to others. You need to be available to your executive managers to inquire, discuss, question, and inform because they ultimately require you to lead.

The P9 Management Model's quick reference guide of relational factors should be the lens you use when considering crucial matters under the Processes Management umbrella.

9

PRODUCTION MANAGEMENT

> *"The way to get started is to quit talking and begin doing."*
> **Walt Disney**

Take a moment to think about what your organisation produces. Ask a customer or a new member of staff to answer that question, and they are likely to list the tangible products known to them that you sell or the services you offer.

A senior manager should answer with a different perspective because they will be thinking about the numerous items produced within their area of responsibility. Yet, most of your organisation's senior managers will not be directly responsible for making a tangible product or service. Yet they will be cognitive of all the items that their team produces. As a result, numerous tasks daily performed by them or their team will contribute to the essential running of your organisation, and each one of these requires some degree of management.

Indeed, it is worth investing a few minutes considering the array of areas, items, procedures and matters that create or add to the production of something within your organisation. Such issues differ depending on your organisation's sector, but listed below are just one hundred matters that would be relevant in all but minor organisations. This list is neither extensive nor collectively exhaustive, but I hope you agree it is a good beginning.

Accounting	Accreditations	Advertising	Alliances	Annual Leave
Appetising (creative ideas for future opportunities)	Associations	Banking	Bookkeeping	Business Development
Career Planning	Cataloguing	Clients	Closing Procedures	Communication
Community Service Leave	Company Returns	Compassionate Leave	Conference planning	Conflict Resolution
Consultants	Corporate Citizenship	Culture Development	Currency Exchange	Customers
Departmental Research & Development	Digitalization	Dispute Resolution	Distribution Channels	E-Commerce
Employee Assistance	Employee Benefits	Employee Data Privacy	External Advisors	Financing
Frameworks	Gender Equality	Governance	Growth Strategies	Hospitality
Human Resource	Inspiration	Insurance	Invoicing	Information Technology
Leases	Legal Compliance	Leverage Opportunities	Licencing	Litigation
Locations	Long service leave	Marketing	Meetings	Motivation
Networking	Onboarding	Opening Procedures	Opening Hours	Operation Manuals
Orders	Ownership	Performance Measurement	People	Planning
Policies	Policy Alignment	Policy Reviews	Positioning	Presentations
Product Design	Product Development	Product Testing	Product Delivery	Product Evaluation
Promotion	Public Holidays	Public Relations	Organisational Purpose	Quality Control

Recruitment	Rental Agreements	Reporting	Research	Risk Management
Rosters	Schedules	Service Delivery	Seminars	Sick Leave
Statements	Strategic Planning	Structure (organisational)	Supply Chains	Synergy Creation
Termination	Training & Development	Transportation	Travel	Utilities

ISSUES LIST 1

As you pursued the above Issue List, I am confident you would have identified items I did not include, either for reading time or space reasons or (quite possibly) because I am unaware of the specific matter. Nevertheless, to varying degrees, each of those listed will involve processes, and, just like a Practices Management item, a process presents opportunities for assessment and refinement. For your organisation to become exceptional, it must have a 'continual improvement of processes' culture.

Processes *create* Production

Without a product, tangible or intangible, your organisation has no long-term future! Indeed your organisation only exists to produce or distribute something. The bottom line is that the better the something or the successful distribution of that something, the better your chances of achieving optimal organisational performance and reaching sustainable excellence.

It is a real challenge to think of something produced that, as a minimum, does not involve a single process. The sum of processes creates the resulting culmination; the product.

The Model respects this reality and encourages, enables and empowers managers to be perpetually mindful of seeking improvements in each creation step. Following are each inter-relational impacts that Production has on its cohort operational elements.

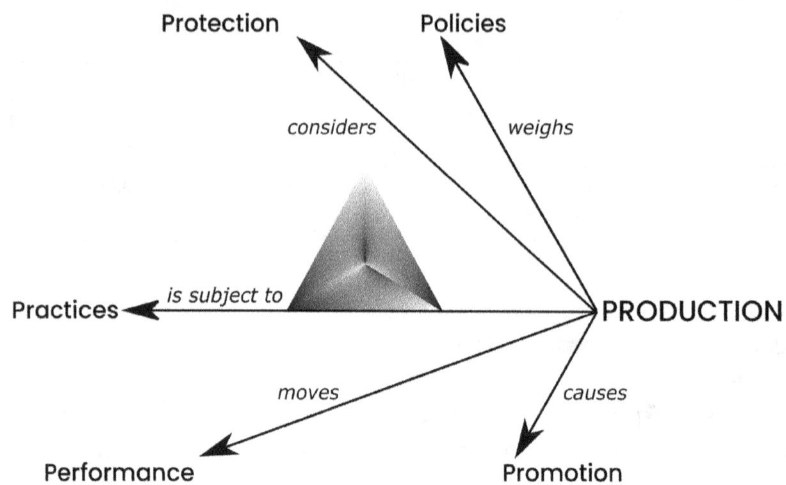

Production *considers* Protection

The phrase, *"there are more ways than one to skin a cat[24]"* is stated to have originated from a short story "The Money Diggers" written by the American author Seba Smith in 1840, where it is stated as; *"There are more ways than one to skin a cat, so are there more ways than one of digging for money."*

The same often applies to your organisation's produced things; *"there is more than one way to produce that"*. There are numerous reasons for this, including technology advancements, alteration or replacement of subject materials, design refinement, additional features, and modified procedures.

Such production changes vary but include external pressures involving marketplace demands, regulatory or legislative changes, and economic, climatic and environmental influences. Having managerial experience and reading the chapter on Protection Management, you can now appreciate The Model assigning Protection with the responsibility of securing and advancing your organisation's purpose for its existence and longevity. Unquestionably, there is also a direct correlation between what

24 Quote | Literary Devices.net - https://literarydevices.net/there-are-more-ways-than-one-to-skin-a-cat/

you produce, its method of production, and your organisation's reputation.

Indeed, you will recall reading, *"If you think of Protection as a boat responsible for keeping the organisation afloat, every time a hole remains unplugged, the organisation is one step closer to sinking."* One such potential *hole* is your Production Management. Thankfully, good governance and conforming staff that understand and value their organisation's *Protection* will respect the imposed governance measures regularly reflected in policies.

Production *weighs* Policies

According to Oxford Languages (OL), ***'weigh'***[25] means *"assess the nature or importance of, especially with a view to a decision or action"*, and OL's definition of ***'assess'***[26] is *"evaluate or estimate the nature, ability, or quality of."*

So applying The Model, one should understand the impacting relationship of Production to Policies as, *Production evaluates or estimates the nature, ability, or quality of the heart or importance of relevant Policies, especially with a view to a decision or action.* Right now, I am guessing you are glad I do not expect you to memorise that detailed definition.

The outworking of this approach is to ensure that everything produced within your organisation, and the methods used to create such, identify and weigh up relevant policies to ensure that the current end product, and the procedures used in its making, are in line with your organisation's policies.

Remember that a policy has three responsibilities:

1. To achieve a purpose that solves a problem or satisfies a need
2. To provide clear direction and guidance
3. To be a final, authoritative point of reference demanding compliance

25 Weigh definition | Oxford Languages - https://www.lexico.com/definition/weigh
26 Assess definition | Oxford Languages - https://www.lexico.com/definition/assess

As an exceptional CEO, your goals will include ensuring every member of your Executive Management Team is fully aware of and agrees with a policy's responsibilities and the process defined as "a sequence of actions or steps undertaken to achieve a particular outcome". The outcome of this will then be threefold:

- The product and its inherent creation procedures are compliant with a policy
- Identifying the need for reviewing a particular policy to reflect a necessary change
- An ongoing focus on continual improvement of your organisation's products and procedures.

Production *moves* Performance

OL's definition for '*move*'[27] is to *"go in a specified direction or manner; change position"*, and its definition of *performance*[28] is *"the action or process of performing a task or function"*. Your objective is to increase (change) your organisation's performance by continually improving the outcomes of each of the six operational elements.

In managing Production, there are two areas of performance that require attention. Firstly and logically, you will positively *move* (increase) profitability by improving the methods of producing a product, including:

- Reducing the total timeline by refining the sequence of procedures
- Minimising materials used without diminishing quality
- Reducing production costs
- (where appropriate) increasing the sale price due to additional features or a significant product quality increase

27 Move definition | Oxford Languages - https://www.lexico.com/definition/move

28 Performance definition | Oxford Languages - https://www.lexico.com/definition/performance

Then secondly, by improving all the involved individuals' performances (from concept, planning and design to end product completion and delivery).

In a focused can-do culture, it is common to observe how improvements in the production process or the progress of the end product's functionality, or quality, motivate those involved individuals to shoot for additional enhancements, particularly when they receive appropriate recognition for doing so.

Production is *subject to* Practices

This declaration of the relationship between Production and Practices reflects reality and further confirms the collaboration between Production Management and Practices Management.

Remember (OL's) definition of Practice[29], *"the actual application or use of an idea, belief, or method, as opposed to theories relating to it."*

Thomas Edison[30] "is the world gold standard for invention, innovation, and entrepreneurship. No one has ever duplicated the sheer volume and depth of his 1,093 patents, virtually defining

29 Practice definition | Oxford Languages - https://www.lexico.com/definition/practice
30 Thomas Edison - https://www.thomasedison.org/all-about-tom

the standard of living we enjoy today. He invented both products and systems to support those products. His classic inventions were the phonograph, the electric light bulb, the electric power industry and motion pictures. LIFE magazine named him The Man of the Millennium."

In an often-quoted interview that raised his failures, Thomas Edison stated: "I have not failed 10,000 times—I've successfully found 10,000 ways that will not work." There is ongoing disagreement about how many attempts it took before the electric light globe was a marketable product. Edison was much more than an inventor. Again quoting from the Edison Innovation Foundation, "Thomas Edison went on to systematise the process of invention, transforming it from a cottage industry into an industrial powerhouse that led to the modern-day concept of R&D labs in most Fortune 500 companies. Some would say this was his greatest invention, codifying the process of invention, allowing industry to continue indefinitely, and scientifically, the American Industrial Revolution of the late 1800s."

A modern-day product example is a lithium-ion battery. These now power motor vehicles and a multitude of other items. NASA developed one of the battery's earliest examples in 1965. Of course, today, these batteries are commonplace. Global lithium-ion battery production capacity predictions for the 2023 range are from 400 to 1,100 gigawatt-hours.

There is a timeframe similarity between the 'development to commercialisation' history of the electric light globe and the lithium-ion battery. Through constant research and development, various entities progressed their reliability, performance, and usability.

Competent managers know that anything produced can be improved by refining the sequential methods utilised. You also understand that most production changes derive from a performance-based focus on production times, material costs and quality outcomes. Again, your responsibility is to create a culture that encourages and rewards participation in continual improvement.

Production *causes* Promotion

OL's definition of *cause*[31] is *"a principle, aim, or movement to which one is committed and which one is prepared to defend or advocate"*.

As with all things that management is responsible for, promotion needs to be strategic. Whatever your organisation produces that benefits its intended users (which, for this explanation, I will call the primary product) requires a purposeful commitment to effectively promoting the product. As a result, an additional production step supersedes the primary product's production, causing the creation of a promotional component.

The type, style and budget for such promotion will vary depending upon the product's positioning, internal or external. For example, a change informing of additional EOTF (End Of Trip Facilities) is likely to be a memo, a poster, and a mention in your organisation's E-news with little or no budget. The opposite would be launching a new prime product or service, which will incur significant attention and require a significant budget (possibly even a seven-digit one).

> **R.Q.** *Concerning something currently produced that benefits internal usage, what promotional policies, systems, and reviews are apparent in your organisation? **W.I.D.***

Production Management Summary

Should it be argued that, within The Model, **Production** is the *make or break* operation element?

The short answer is no. As earlier stated when explaining The Model, *"Each one is a 'heavy lifter'; whose objectives are clear and measurable, whose performance needs to be consistently high, and whose contribution deserves organisational-wide respect, indeed, to be honoured."* However, several managers have expressed that

31 Cause definition | Oxford Languages - https://www.lexico.com/definition/cause

'make or break' thought, indicating the marketplace's estimated importance of conquering Production Management.

Production Management is the most procedurally based element. The production of something, birthed from either an idea or a need, quickly includes numerous procedures. Each step should then be open to regular analysis and potential improvement. Only on rare occasions does the saying *"if it isn't broke, don't fix it"* have real-world reality. The continual improvement approach mainly occupies the person's mind primarily responsible for Production, thus ensuring the performance and quality of a product.

Production Management is undeniably and indisputably the area of responsibility that requires the most significant investment of your team's time. This statement is factual unless your organisation is (exclusively) a reseller or only a redistributor. Your product is the primary window through which your customers/clients view you, so you need to get it (and keep it) right.

10

PROMOTION MANAGEMENT

> *"Don't blame the marketing department. The buck stops with the chief executive."*
> **John D. Rockefeller**

Wow, we have arrived. The Model's ninth element is the sixth and final of the operational elements; the **Promotion** element. In the chapter where I explained The Model, you read, *"It does not represent specific divisions or departments but critical areas of management responsibility. Indeed, it is likely that every division or department will engage with and utilise each 'P' element."*

In your journey of understanding The Model to date, I am sure you can see the intent and agree with the accuracy of those two above statements. Each one is truly critical to your organisation's overall performance. Of course, each operational element will have its challenging moments in the spotlight under specific circumstances. On such occasions, the management of each will experience being determinedly:

- Tested for it being:
    - Fit for purpose
    - Robust
    - Effective

- Thoroughly scrutinised
- Critically evaluated.

This approach is crucial when sustainable excellence is the target. Highly successful organisations will not tolerate mediocrity. As one of their core values, such organisations include creating, implementing, and monitoring the highest standards.

For almost anything to have benefit, it must be made known! The enduring challenge for those responsible for Promotion Management remains in the questions of:

- What needs to be made known?
- Why is it essential for it to be made known?
- When must it be made known?
- Where must it be made known?
- Who must make it known? And
- How is it to be made known?

Promotion can significantly influence the purposeful success of a particular product or service that your organisation relies upon for profitability or survival.

I have long thought that Promotion's objective is simply publicising an item or matter that you desire a target group to be fully aware of, including its purpose and benefits. Promotion refers to the complete collection of activities communicating the procedure, product, brand, service, item or matter to the targeted user/s. The idea is to make as many people as necessary aware of your *thing*, attract them to your *thing*, and induce them to buy (or buy into) your *thing* in preference over the offerings of alternatives.

However, The P9 Management Model's Think Big focus advocates that Promotion Management is far broader than advertising and marketing. My career experience leads me to agree with John D. Rockefeller's quote above. Ultimately, the responsibility for the quality, performance and direction of your organisation's Marketing Department lies with you, the CEO.

Naturally, it would be preferable if you were across both external and internal promotional activities and, where appropriate, make your appraisal comments known.

You won't necessarily create or execute most of (or perhaps any of) such activities, but every manager in your organisation will know your communication standards and preferences. For instance, regarding external stakeholders, the desired modes, styles and objectives of any direct communication with a customer/client, distribution channel contact, external contractor, or adviser will reflect your Core Values Statement.

The same principles apply to internal communication with appropriate variations to directness and expectations.

Of course, many matters (mainly internal) that require communication need only the inclusion of bare facts. Nevertheless, many of these will still need promotion (even if that is just a notification) to ensure they are effectively received, read, understood, and acted upon within the desired timeline. However, it falls under Promotion Management when these include a reason, justification, or benefit.

Sadly, Promotion Management's focus remains almost exclusively external in many organisations.

Given the vast array of expertise, education and easily accessible information available in the marketplace, plus what I have contributed throughout this book, I choose not to include every marketing type, theory, model, and template. The same goes for Communication and Public Relations. A timely reminder from my Preface, *"One book does not make us an expert; this only happens when one has a significant measure of both knowledge and experience."*

Historically, few executives from a marketing background ended up sitting behind the CEO's desk, but there are signs of change. In 2018 CEO Today published an article[32] on the evolution of CMOs to CEO positions and, therefore, the next generation of business leaders.

32 CMO to CEO | CEO Today Magazine - https://www.ceotodaymagazine.com/2018/09/why-the-next-wave-of-ceos-will-be-from-marketing/

At the risk of annoying you, I repeat P.T. Barnum, ***"Without promotion, something terrible happens... nothing!"***

Of the thirty-six relational impacts of The P9 Management Model, only five remain to be considered, understood, valued and applied.

As with the proceeding thirty-one impactors, you need to appreciate the position and significant contribution of **Promotion Management.** That will seriously assist you in advancing your organisation's progress towards becoming recognised as achieving exceptional performance and reaching sustainable excellence.

Processes *deploy* Promotion

When reviewing my detailed observations and recalling the various case studies about highly successful organisations, I realised they had one other crucial methodology of unifying differentiators. They had repeatedly honed their processes! Subsequently, they intentionally promoted the end product of those processes and promoted them well.

This intentionality is a top-down strategic determination. As the CEO, you must champion efficient communications and marketing. You must also regularly raise the promotional topics on your radar, holding those appointed accountable to promote whatever is needed and successfully do so.

Hence within The Model, Processes do not just use Promotion; they deploy Promotion! OL's definition for *'deploy'*[33] is to *"move (troops or equipment) into position for military action"*.

This approach is strategic, intentional, proactive, and pre-emptive. Its execution, which is precisely targeted to achieve its objectives and maximise the preferred outcome, adds to your organisation's desired culture.

33 Deploy definition | Oxford Languages - https://www.lexico.com/definition/deploy

Following are the final five *Relational Factors* of The Model. For a CEO to excel, understanding them is equally essential to those relating to the proceeding twenty-five impacting operational relationships.

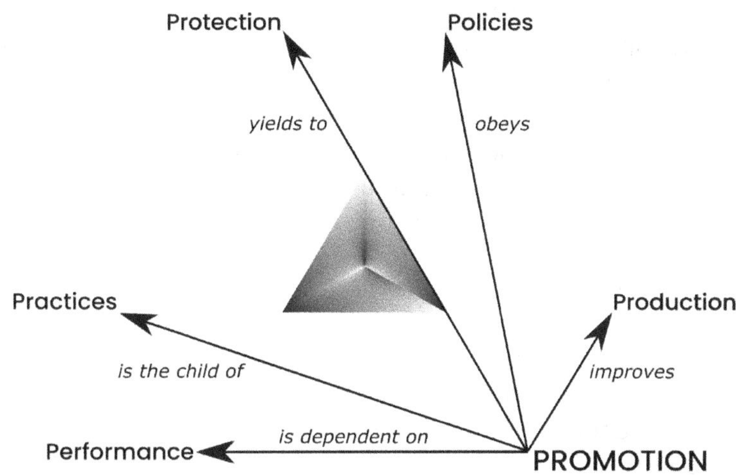

Promotion *yields to* Protection

In the Protection Management chapter, you read, "*The P9 Management Model has carefully identified Promotion as a Processes P because Processes deploy Promotion. Because of promoters' requisite creative and enthusiastic nature, it is the one P that requires constant review; Promotion yields to Protection.*"

Many organisational structures include a CMO (Chief Marketing Officer). The objective of this role is to lead the entity's promotional activities, including market research, brand management, marketing communications, product development and management, customer service, and pricing. The CMO is responsible for managing a team of marketing professionals and reports to the CEO.

These marketing professionals' requisite creative and enthusiastic nature necessitates the relational impact of Promotion to Protection. As the CEO, you also want them to be highly creative, explorative and boundary-stretching. However, these attributes can cause tension between the desire to test the inherent strength of your boundaries; boundaries that were created and honed to protect your organisation's purpose and secure its longevity.

In the absence of a CMO, whoever is responsible for managing the Marketing Team, will ocassionally require them to modify their approach and come back with an acceptable solution. Unless they can prove that a Protection directive has become incorrect or obsolete, they must *yield* to the authority of the Protection measures. Without The Model's paradigm of organisational-wide shared respect, this tension can be disruptive and counterproductive.

Promotion *obeys* Policies

This declaration goes hand in hand with *Promotion yields to Protection* because policies are the vehicle Protection uses to guide and control your organisation's governance. *Obeys*, the descriptive verb is intense and often received as acidic. Indeed, it can be the most effective test of your team leaders' abilities to be P9 knowledgeable and effective communicators.

However, because almost all Protection directives get delivered through policies, it also presents opportunities for testing or filtering a policy's current relevancy, appropriateness and accuracy. You will more than occasionally experience the measure of determination by your marketing professionals to make relevant, helpful and practicable recommendations when challenging the intent or validity of a policy. You will read more regarding these experiences in a later chapter titled The P9 Cohesive Management Culture.

The clear challenge here is to achieve high levels of Promotional performance in conjunction with the essential compliance required by minimalizing tension and disruptive interference. I hope your thinking immediately goes to matters previously covered in Practices Management that would provide direction and present solutions.

Promotion is *the child of* Practices

You know that Promotion is a 'Processes' operational element, and Practices is a 'People' operational element. Generally (although in some instances, A.I. now plays a role), people create processes, and then those processes are either performed by more people or are automated by machinery.

In the context of The P9 Management Model, I describe Practices as *"what individuals do and how they do it"*. Although to fully appreciate and agree with the descriptive words of Promotion → Practices, consider the following three OL definitions of the crucial words used.

1. Promotion[34]; is an *"activity that supports or encourages a cause, venture, or aim."*
2. 'child of'[35]; *"a person regarded as the product of (a specified influence or environment)."*
3. Practices[36]; *"the actual application or use of an idea, belief, or method, as opposed to theories relating to it."*

So one could express the descriptive phrase of Promotion → Practices as, *Promotion is the activity that supports or encourages a cause, venture, or aim as if undertaken by the specified influence, and regarded as the product of the actual application or use of an idea, belief, or method, as opposed to theories relating to it.*

However, I prefer to remember it as simply Promotion *is the child of* Practices. The choice of the word *child* needs to be clarified before someone takes offence. **Let me be obvious here; I do not consider marketing professionals as children.** I am only referring to the Promotion element within The Model, specifically its relationship to the Practices element.

Interestingly, however, I recall reading more than one survey that showed the practices (*what individuals do and how they do it*) of

34 Promotion definition | Oxford Languages - https://www.lexico.com/definition/promotion

35 'Child of' definition | Oxford Languages - https://www.lexico.com/definition/child

36 Practices definition | Oxford Languages - https://www.lexico.com/definition/practices

individuals responsible for promotional activities often included the following characteristics:

- Are eager to experience, learn, and acquire skills
- Love stories and have rich imaginations
- Enjoy singing, acting and being creative
- Want good to triumph over evil
- Are above average at memorising

Promotional Management must encourage and motivate these characteristics within the Marketing Team to ensure that the best results occur. The bottom line is that to improve your organisation's promotional performance, you must enhance the practices of all those involved.

Promotion is *dependent* on Performance

By now, you understand the irrefutable reliance of Promotion has on People's two operational elements; Practices and Performance. The strength of the relationship between these two is the closest of all three paired operational elements. Married to the *'impact of Practices'* is the *'effect of Performance'* on Promotion, and it is a marriage of equal opportunity. Each contributes directly to creating, developing, testing, and reviewing promotional material.

The one named *Practices* is known for its actual practicality. It is essential. Nevertheless, the other, called *Performance,* determines the execution and result of Promotion. Some might see Practices as the head and Performance as the neck, which turns the head anyway it wants to; (yes, I know it is a line from the original *'My Big Fat Greek Wedding'*). Forgive my amateurish attempt to use a little literacy licence. Only, I want to make this subject's relational impact declaration straightforward. If you insist on continually experiencing high-quality and highly effective promotional material (and you should), your organisation needs to manage each person's performance in the entire process.

Typically, that responsibility rests on the shoulders of the Team Leaders of those creating promotional material. They must continually observe behaviour, language, negativity, disheartenment, and potential or actual tensions, acting promptly, if necessary, to rectify any counter-productive matter.

This responsibility is crucial within Promotion Management, whether the specific promotion is internally or externally focused. The actions, urgency and impacts may differ, but both focuses require dedicated attention.

Promotion *improves* Production

Well done, reader; you are now exploring the final relational impact of The Model. Marketing professionals love this declaration because it confirms their worth.

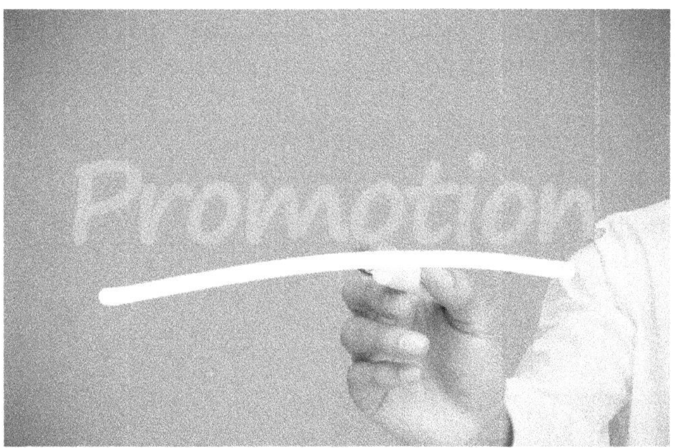

The specialisation area of marketing research is a science far too sophisticated to explore and fully comprehend within the pages of this book. There is no lack of valuable information available to those who seek to increase their knowledge and skillsets. For advanced levels of understanding, I recommend you look at work published by veterans like Alvin C, Burns, Ronald F. Bush and Ann Veeck (authors of the *Marketing Research*[37] excellent series of books, now in its 9th edition).

37 Marketing Research, Global Edition | Marketing Research | Marketing | Business & Economics | Store | Learner AU Site (pearson.com)

Before creating a marketing plan for a new-to-market product (or product range), your marketing experts, hopefully included from as early as conception, will insist on performing relevant research to establish (as a minimum):

- Competition
- Demand
- Launch timing
- Position
- Predicted life-cycle and predicted phases
- Pricing
- Promotional strategies
- Target demographics

Your marketing team will also, having conducted qualitative reviews and identifying new opportunities, make recommendations for:

- Modifications to the subject product's performance and features
- Additional features
- Improving user manuals
- New products

Promotion Management Summary

Promoting products, services, or other matters of significant importance within your organisation is not optional; it is compulsory, essential, and performance-critical.

The business realm is possibly the most complex of all environments. In the Marketing area alone, there are numerous components, including:

- Consumer behaviour
- Content Plans & Schedules
- Goals & Objectives

- Marketing management
- Marketing mix
- Marketing research
- Marketing strategy
- Metrics
- Pricing
- Product management
- Promotional Planning
- Target Audience

Then add to those components the vast array of models, theories, acronyms and accompanying advertising-specific jargon, and one finds themself in a sea of new literacy. While the above highlights its exclusivity and complexity, conquering the wild matrix of promotional activities pays rich dividends to its players; think of the world's two most prominent and valuable technology companies[38], Apple and Samsung.

Say you are the new CEO or a member of your organisation's Executive Management Team and have not risen from a marketing career. You will know that even a recent marketing graduate, who has just joined your organisation's marketing team as a junior member, will be more knowledgeable. Therefore, you have three additional responsibilities.

Firstly, ensure that those, who report to you on promotional matters, are the best marketplace available and suitably professional managers, meeting your chosen standards and ensuring they are also the right fit for your organisation's culture.

Secondly, you must be confident that they receive a full briefing on all relevant and necessary details to produce promotional plans and perform subsequent actions.

---

38 Accurate at the time of writing this chapter.

Finally, when they report to you on their promotional projects, be convinced of the validity of the information provided in the context of the bigger picture that your elevated position grants you. I am not suggesting that you question its authenticity (*"Houston, we have a problem"* if you need to do that). That manager will impress you with their assurance of the recommendations presented being the best option. However, you should apply The P9 Management Model mindset and consider the impact of the advice on the other five operational elements.

The bottom line in Promotion Management, hire the best experts and extract the best results they can produce for you.

R.Q. *After reading this chapter on Promotion Management, what matters of concern do you have?* ***W.I.D.***

11

ENLIGHTENING ALIGNMENT

> *"Words without action are like wheels without traction."*
> **Russell Driscoll**

In the chapter describing The Model, I asked, *"What is the power of The P9 Management Model?"*

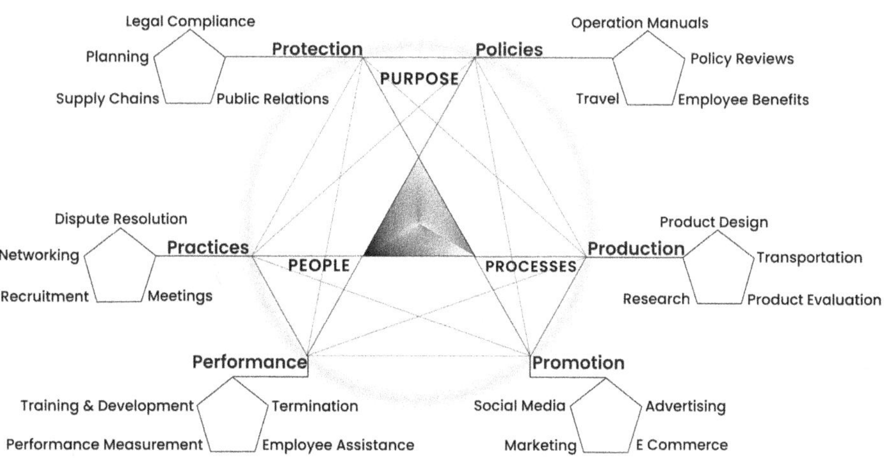

You will recall I advocated that: *"To achieve Organisational Excellence, you must ensure that these six operational elements,*

Protection, Policies, Product, Promotion, Performance and Practices, are correctly aligned, equally valued, and all achieve their objective purpose."

"This measure of Organisational Excellence is assessed by systematically analysing their performance and relative contribution using values 1 through 9, where 1 represents 'poor performance' and 9 means 'outstanding performance'. Each element has different factors that require assessment, which can vary between organisations."

In this chapter, I will share some thoughts and methods to assist you in achieving Enlightening Alignment. This phrase, *Enlightening Alignment*, if adopted and repeatedly used by you, are the two words that will form an organisation-wide cohesive mantra. Over time you will discover that this catchphrase will instantly bring a laser-like focus to a specific matter, minimising confusion, enabling subject-relevant clarity, eliminating distraction, empowering engagement, and producing positive results. Also, in this chapter, I will answer some common questions when discussing The Model with senior managers.

In my Preface, I stated, ' *The book is not a quick fix motivational text'* and *'Nor will reading this book guarantee* you instant success.' After ten chapters of reading, in conjunction with your contemplations, questions, reflections and analysis, I hope you now consider The P9 Management Model to be as much about philosophy as it is about structure.

Two additional critical components, *Decision Making* and *Culture*, introduced in later chapters, work with and form part of The Model's philosophical approach. Without these other components, one could argue that The Model is just another theory.

> ***Sideline**: You may have noticed the disproportional space given to each core element (together with their operational elements) and concluded that I do not consider them to deserve equal recognition and value. You're mistaken if you believe that conclusion. Still, your observation of disproportional space is accurate. As I progressed through the three core elements of Purpose, People, and Processes, there was a word reduction of approximately thirty per cent for each. These reductions were not a*

reflection of equality but rather a result of my experience. Let me explain by beginning with Processes.

This book is a construct of observations and studies. Naturally, my professional experience has included numerous conversations with senior managers. I understand that you, as a senior manager, are already a specialist or (perhaps even) an expert in a particular discipline or skill set, educated, qualified and experienced, which has enabled you to succeed and achieve elevation. You are a competent producer of something or many things. Therefore, you should know all the departmental matters covered by the 'Processes' element. Remember, The Model offers an alternative ideology structure and an altered paradigm. It is about areas of responsibility, not specific tasks or departments. My objective was twofold:

1. *To inform you of its (Processes) position*
2. *To inform you of 'Processes' relationship to its two operational elements of Production and Promotion and their relational impacts on the other operational elements*

Next, the People chapters' increased content reflects the reality of management time investment. A century of business case studies measuring Time and Motion to improve productivity show senior managers spending up to seventy per cent of their working days with other people. Most senior managers spend less than thirty per cent of their time working alone, usually when working from home or in transit. There have been many models and recommended practices of how a senior manager should divide their work time. Steven Covey introduced one popular prioritisation concept named 'The Four Quadrants of Time Management' when he first published his best-selling book titled 'The 7 Habits of Highly Effective People[39]' in 1989. You will find a myriad of Time Management ideologies in the marketplace and academic circles. The content in this book's People chapters highlighted the consistent aspects of individuals and teams in high-performing organisations run by exceptional leaders. Such entities focus on extracting the most significant outputs within a non-exploitatory environment that, at every opportunity, optimised staff satisfaction levels.

Finally, there is far too little material, by any considered measure, in the marketplace on Organisational Purpose. Sadly, too many organisations have failed or remained below par because they lacked a well-defined, authentic, and convictional purpose. Therefore, I thought it essential to

39 The 7 Habits of Highly Effective People | Stephen R. Covey - https://www.simonandschuster.com/books/The-7-Habits-of-Highly-Effective-People/Stephen-R-Covey/9781982137137#

> *present a comprehensive introductory overview before describing the seven components of Purpose Management that I initially identified and have since further developed. It may surprise you that many senior managers have never heard someone speak, with authority, on Organisational Purpose. Consequently, I certainly do not apologise for giving Purpose Management forty per cent more space than People Management, which gained forty-five per cent more than Processes Management.*
>
> *Again, I assure you that there is prerequisite equality of recognition and value across all three core elements of Purpose, People and Processes.*

For the balance of this chapter, I will briefly respond to a few frequently asked questions about implementing The P9 Management Model.

Managing Purpose, People, and Processes, through the equilateral triangular hub lens will be crucial in personalising your approaches to the following five questions:

- How do you get there?
- Why is there no user-ready and easy *'off the shelf'* solution to analysing and measuring operational **P**s?
- Who will do *What*?
- What are the early steps?
- Where does it end?

How do you get there?

The goal is to align these nine elements to fulfil their objectives.

Firstly, the core elements of Purpose, People, and Processes, that form the hub must become firmly planted in your mind as the cornerstone areas of focus within your organisation.

How should I decide on a systematic approach for each operational element?

Great question because you now appreciate that each element is unique in its characteristics and idiosyncrasies.

Then beyond every operational element being unique, their specific components in levels below each element differ, depending on your organisation's type, size, and structure. Indeed, even organisations within the same sector will likely require different measurements for different areas.

As the CEO, you will have particular preferences and priorities, including modes, methods, and sophistication levels, and rightfully so. It is your gig. You are the driver held responsible for achieving high and sustainable success.

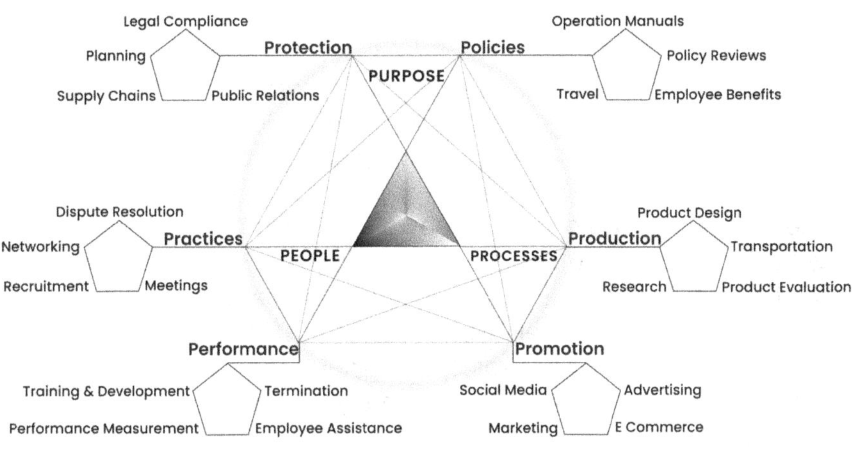

I recommend you take a 'step by step' and *'level by level'* approach. Begin by deciding which operational element you would first develop, e.g. Policies, Practices or Promotion. To shorten the development timeline of the first element chosen, I recommend choosing the one where you are the most experienced and confident.

Then, identify each area you determine is crucial to measure within that element's coverage (refer to The Model's expanded view for ideas). For example, If you chose the *Promotion* element, you might first focus on eCommerce. Next, identify the touchpoints (within eCommerce) you believe are the best performance indicators. They may include any or all of the following:

- Average order value
- Cart abandonment rate
- Checkout abandonment rate
- Conversion rate
- Cost per acquisition
- Customer lifetime value
- Gross margin
- Revenue gained on advertising spent

You will already have established analytics of performance indicators in numerous management areas. Unless you are dissatisfied with those indicators, their inclusion makes sense until they prove inadequate or unsuitable.

The next step would usually be to determine the mode. Most senior managers are reasonably comfortable using dashboards on their monitors. Because of their popularity and relatively short development timelines, dashboards create a uniformity of presentation across all areas and elements. So, dashboards may prove to be your preference. Alternately, you might prefer to view reports.

Then it would help if you determined a rationale for calculating the results. So, still using the eCommerce example, you might use the weighted average method to represent a collective conclusion (more on this topic in a moment). Some managers will focus more on *Average order value* and *Gross margin*. In contrast, others will choose *Customer lifetime value* and *Revenue on advertising spent* or other options. Your choice will depend on the factors you determine are crucial to your organisation.

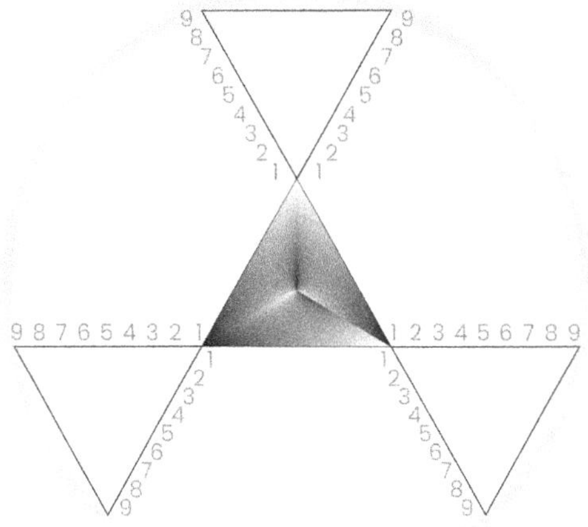

Having built an index for each area within each contributing component, you can create an overall index for the relevant operational element. In the example used above, that would be *Promotion*.

The other Processes operational element is *Production*. Use similarly styled but unique measures for its indicators to create its index. You could then use the same approach to build an index for their parent core element, again being (in this case) Processes. While there are many options available for calculating the data from these components, remember the prime factor is that the six operational elements of The Model must use a 1 to 9 final measurement to produce an accurate picture of your organisation's overall performance.

Once you have completed the above-described procedures for all six operational elements, the final development step is **The P9 Excellence Index**. You will be delighted to know that final index is the quickest step. The P9 Excellence Index measures all elements' performance, as in the example following.

Having reached this level (or perhaps during the process), you may find this an area where your Board of Directors want direct involvement, particularly when determining the final weightings. Weightings? Yes. Having chosen the components you want to measure, you (or your Board) might wish (for varying reasons) to give more prominence to one or more of the components you measure. A cautionary note: This requires wisdom and integrity not to grant a higher weighting to your better performing (or underperforming) components to lift that element's rating. Always remember your endgame goal; sustainable excellence. Also, remember help is available.

The above-described process (also) produces its best outcomes when the executive management team is involved. The process benefits from a universal agreement of components to be measured and the weightings used.

Naturally, indexes and dashboards are not the only modes you can develop or adapt to suit your specific requirements. Based on your confidence in suitability, user-friendliness, and performance, the criteria of your last mode choice will likely be familiar to you.

Why is there no easy-to-use, off-the-shelf solution to analysing and measuring operational Ps?

We are not discussing an organisation's calendar, staff roster or accounting system, so this answer is self-evident. You know that your organisation is not a clone of a competitor. You also understand that all the operational elements that require final measurement are umbrella areas of responsibility, not just previously recognised tasks. So, the choice of their contributing components are organisation specific, and their factors measured vary immensely, depending upon your priorities and preferences.

You drive this process and determine its priorities, measurement methods, and systematic approach. Just as you have established analytics of performance indicators in other management areas, you have also found your preferred ways of reviewing and monitoring that would adapt to The Model. Unsurprisingly, and as mentioned, many of you prefer to use dashboards as an efficient and productive way of handling specific matters daily.

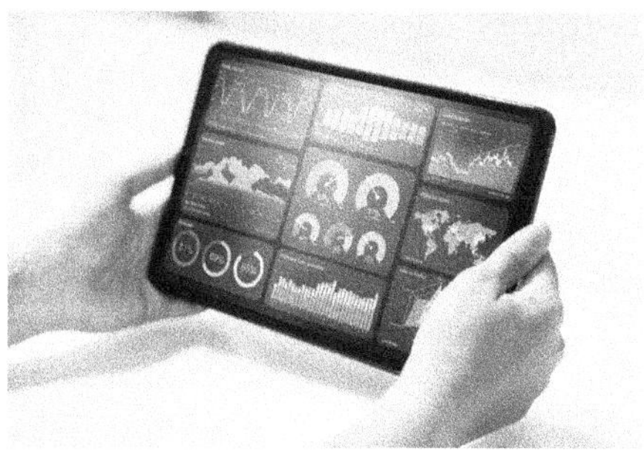

The marketplace offers several generic dashboard templates. Nevertheless, I have begun writing specifications for developing indexes that allow users to choose from a select number of everyday items, input their individual choices, and then determine each weight. I also intend to write specifications for developing suitable dashboard templates. While the inherent items list could grow almost endlessly, together with the philosophical approach to determining the weightings, I strongly recommend that you begin with a modest number and then, one level at a time, build on it. This method will deliver clarity and confidence, checking it against your *gut* sense.

Who will do What?

It starts with you, the CEO, the leader. Begin by preparing yourself for change. Your confidence in The Model needs to be at the level where your desire compels you to begin your journey to becoming a P9 Management Model Graduate. Believing in its credibility and value is not anywhere near enough. You need to own it before you can drive it! You need to have some vision of a destination before describing it to others.

Again, remember what you are aiming for here; exceptional performance and sustainable excellence. This goal elevates you from average into exclusive minority territory. You will join the realm of the *all-stars*. You remain the pilot while I help navigate the course (if you choose). I am introducing you to the tools and a philosophical approach essential to propel your organisation forward, but the wheel and the throttle are in your hands and control. You determine the direction, the waypoints and the rate of acceleration. You wanted the role; now live it.

The bottom line is this, you are the driver, but you're not a sole trader. A sole trader needs the motivation to get up each morning and do all it takes to get the job done. In contrast, you lead an organisation with a team of competent and hopefully motivated managers. What they require is an authentic sense of inspiration; in bucketloads. They need ongoing confidence in your capacity to lead and overcome obstacles. They need to believe that you are courageous while also balanced, having the strengths of being reliable, considered, and wise. They need you to be dangerously contagious with a definite purpose, appropriate priorities, a supportive mentality, and unwavering determination. Why? Because they become the co-owners and the implementors of change.

In The P9 Management Model styled organisation, you sow the seeds, but there is shared responsibility for achieving the objectives and delivering the harvest. The first level of sharing must be with your Executive Management Team. As previously suggested, engage them early.

Once you have successfully (through collaboration) developed the strategy, including directional waypoints, areas of measurement and selected indicators, and desired timelines, you are ready to introduce other people within your organisation to the change.

Initially, this phase is more about imagery and direction than detail. You and your executive team have been working on the strategy for months, but it will be big news to them. Now it is time to create an organisation-wide appetite for change. It needs to be sold, not just told. Sell the vision and give them confidence that you and your Executive Management Team have (also) continuously worked on the mission details because history shows they need both. They need to believe that the proposed changes will mean they will work smarter, not harder, and there will be more inclusion.

Remember what is at stake? You will not be speaking about this year's targets, a new product line, or similar. You will be introducing them to something that will change their work world. The P9 Management Model styled organisation becomes the exceptional workplace. They will experience a whole new culture. Indeed, they will build an entirely different culture. Their participation is not optional; it is critically and fundamentally essential!

Nevertheless, it still starts with you, the CEO, the leader.

What are the early steps?

Having decided to become exceptional through utilising The Model, start by regularly introducing into conversations and meetings words of The P9 Primary Mantra *"A worthy & defined Purpose delivered by valued **People** utilising highly developed **Processes** = organisational success leading to sustainable excellence!"*. Of course, feel free to craft it in your own words while covering each crucial component with equal intent, credibility and value.

Increase the opportunities, within your Executive Management Team, for more *Blue-Sky thinking*. I regularly say, *"lose the box"*. Let's think way beyond, way outside our present position and circumstances. Remove the constraints of our present physicality and fill our lungs with the oxygen of some high-altitude air.

1. What would it look like?
2. Who will benefit?
3. What could it achieve?
4. Together, who can we become?

As with any change management matter, you must carefully develop a strategic plan for such change. In the earlier chapter on Purpose Management, I referred to the work of the Andersons and their book ***Beyond Change Management***[40].

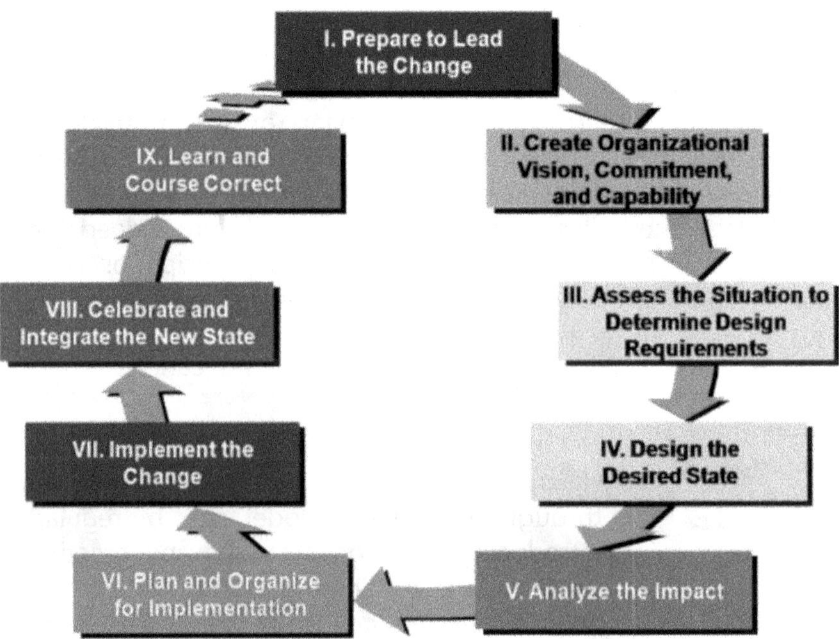

The book includes 'The Change Leader's Roadmap', a systematic approach to navigating the change cycle. Once you have heard the wake-up call, the roadmap's first stage is *'Prepare to Lead*

---

40 Beyond Change Management | Dean Anderson, Linda Ackerman Anderson - https://www.wiley.com/en-au/Beyond+Change+Management%3A+How+to+Achieve+Breakthrough+Results+Through+Conscious+Change+Leadership%2C+2nd+Edition-p-9780470891131

Change'. It then advances through the other eight phases of the cycle's lifespan to ensure the best outcomes.

Whatever change management tools, structures and templates you use, ensure that at least all the stages represented in Anderson's roadmap are sufficiently covered.

Having heard the wake-up call, introduced some new language, and decided to become a P9 Management Model-styled organisation, you need to flick the light switch on and enlighten your executive team about the upcoming changes.

You know your team, their behaviour profiles, and their typical reactions to change. Don't be surprised if some are at either end of the reaction scale. Some might have been there for a while and display notable enthusiasm. Some might have arrived at where you now think and stand. Others may believe that we are doing ok as an organisation, so why suddenly change? If there has not been frequent or at least occasional discussion about your organisation being average, then talk of change will seem irregular, strange, and even bewildering.

Next, choose how you will introduce and educate your team about the structure and philosophical approach of The Model. You might decide to go it alone; you know The Model and have read about some of its philosophy. Alternately, you could introduce the philosophical approach mixed with a brief overview of The Model's nine elements as areas of responsibility, and then plan a group session with me, the creator of it all, to explore and discuss, in considerably more detail, its power and potential.

You need to assess what amount of your time each executive team member will likely require and subsequently input that into the timeline of your plan. Leadership is about leading, but research (and common sense) shows that tangible demonstrations of respect and appreciation, including one-on-one discussion, produce better senior management-level outcomes.

However, suppose you are committed (wholeheartedly) to the cause. In that case (at some point), that reluctant person will have to indicate that they are on your bus or choose to leave. This situation may cause you some short-term grief. Still, even a competent, experienced, and well-performing individual who cannot adapt to this new direction will now prove to be counter-productive, causing tension and distraction. They must not be allowed, let alone empowered, to restrain your progress, even if they previously held your respect and were considered valuable to the team.

Another step essential to early progress is to use, in everyday conversation, as many of The P9 Management Model's quick reference guide's 36 relationship phrases as possible, without them becoming ridiculous. It is not mandatory to have everyone memorise them, but regularly referring to them reiterates their relevance and focus. Until such time it takes for each executive team member to experience the powerful truth of each relationship, regularly utilising them when illustrating a point or connecting them to a discussed outcome will reinforce their importance in your now changing culture.

Relational Factors of The P9 Management Model

			#		#		#		#		#	
CORE		**Purpose →**	1	***merits*** Protection	2	***drives*** Policies		*A worthy & defined **Purpose** delivered by valued **People** utilising highly developed **Processes** = organisational success leading to sustainable excellence!*				
		People →	3	***perform*** Practices	4	***determine*** Performance						
		Processes →	5	***create*** Production	6	***deploy*** Promotion						
OPERATIONAL	**PURPOSE {**	**Protection →**	7	***steers*** Policies	8	***reviews*** Practices	9	***enhances*** Performance	10	***guides*** Production	11	***monitors*** Promotion
		Policies →	12	***reflect*** Protection	13	***influence*** Practices	14	***affect*** Performance	15	***guard*** Production	16	***regulate*** Promotion
	PEOPLE {	**Practices →**	17	***raise*** Protection	18	***strengthen*** Policies	19	***impact*** Performance	20	***shape*** Production	21	***control*** Promotion
		Performance →	22	***submits to*** Protection	23	***shadows*** Policies	24	***follows*** Practices	25	***supports*** Production	26	***stimulates*** Promotion
	PROCESSES {	**Production →**	27	***considers*** Protection	28	***weighs*** Policies	29	***is subject to*** Practices	30	***moves*** Performance	31	***causes*** Promotion
		Promotion →	32	***yields to*** Protection	33	***obeys*** Policies	34	***is a child of*** Practices	35	***is dependent on*** Performance	36	***improves*** Production

Beyond you and your executive team members becoming knowledgeable of and committed to the objectives of The Model, the balance of non-executive managers needs a similar but less intense level of preparation and education before any formal announcements.

Finally, the last information phase to additional, or all your staff, is discretionary, and you would have already determined its value and appropriateness for your organisation. Suppose you desire to share certain aspects of The Model with all your teams, irrespective of position. Your strategy could include some preliminary teasers, such as creating new posters that suggest something good is about to happen and introducing some relevant information emojis. These tasks are part of creating an organisation-wide appetite for change.

When do you see the benefits?

Benefits! We all want to see them. You and your team have spent months developing and implementing the abovementioned steps. You have invested considerable time, money, mind space, and emotions into making this a reality. So when do you see the benefits? The answer to this question is subject to the following:

- You, as the CEO, will relentlessly demonstrate your absolute confidence in changing your organisation from what it has been to become a wholly different entity on a journey towards exceptional performance and sustainable excellence
- The amount of adequate preparation that you and your executive management team have completed before the launch and implementation of The Model, notably the completeness of the strategic plan
- The initial responses of the majority of your staff will reflect their belief in you and your Executive Management Team
- The *'no turning back, it's all in'* launch campaign and the first year's *'actions, not just words'* will signal the depth of your commitment and the expected longevity of determination to reach the exceptional

There is no *'one fits all'* answer to this subject question. Many variables can determine what your organisation will experience. Many will be within your control, while others, mainly external factors out of leftfield, could constrain your desired outcome. Such negatively impacting factors need to form part of the contingencies section of your strategic plan.

Nevertheless, if you implement all that The Model recommends, there are certain benefits you should anticipate:

- A fresh sense of optimism and enthusiasm within your Executive Management Team
- An improved level of job applicants
- An organisation-wide increase of a *'we can do this better'* mentality
- Enhanced creativity
- Higher levels of staff job satisfaction through a larger sense of inclusion
- Improved governance
- Increased staff-initiated participation
- Sharpened performance.

Naturally, reading one book can never guarantee instant success, but reading it and adopting its contents gives you an unparalleled opportunity to impact your organisation positively.

Where does it end?

Congratulations, you have now completed the reading of ten explanatory chapters of The Model. You have gained more knowledge, formed more views, and created for yourself a new opportunity.

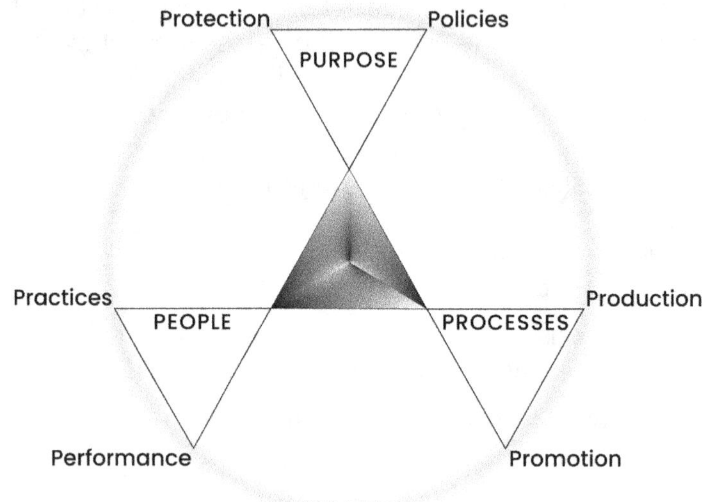

I presume you have heard the phrase 'Knowledge itself is Power'. Those were words written in a book titled 'Meditationes Sacrae' (1597) authored by philosopher and statesman Francis Bacon[41] before becoming the Attorney General and later, the Lord Chancellor of England. Some commentators suggest that he wanted to communicate that having and sharing knowledge increases one's reputation and influence, thereby delivering power.

Bacon's expressed view seems rational, specifically if one interprets power as being personally beneficial. Not wanting to appear arrogant or superior, it is just that in my experience, **only applied knowledge is power**. It is what you do with what you know!

So,

- What will you do with this newly acquired knowledge?
- How will you apply it?
- Who will it benefit?
- Who will you **empower** with it?

41 Fancis Bacon | Wikipedia - https://en.wikipedia.org/wiki/Francis_Bacon

Your answers to those last four questions will determine the answer to the subject question, Where does it end?

Will it become another theory you have studied but do not expect to use? Naturally, if your answer is *Yes* or *Probably*, I would consider that a tragedy because, as my Introduction stated, *"I am inspired by what organisations contribute and achieve for their staff, stakeholders, communities, and occasionally beyond their nation."* If you choose to become a P9 Management Model Graduate, I expect your organisation's contribution will considerably increase.

You are now only three chapters away from finishing reading this book. However, the following three chapters are crucial to success. They are the differentiators between additional knowledge and success. So far, I have mainly focused on the practical daily components of management. What follows focuses on your cognitive approach, culture building, and character attributes.

This book has so far delivered an alternative structured and philosophical management approach. I was upfront about the type of reader I was targeting when I wrote, *"The reader I seek will already be serious about management and leadership"*. I didn't want people to waste their time on a book they had an indifferent approach to. The fact that you are still reading proves that you are indeed that person; alternatively, you could have severe insomnia. I can't help you with the latter.

When asked the subject question, *"Where does it end?"* The answer is that the journey does not end until you retire as a CEO or give up.

You are endlessly learning, growing, and seeking to improve yourself and your organisation in your quest to become exceptional. Of course, many other questions exist for those curious about The Model: How, Why, Who, What, When, and Where. However, instead of reading pages of questions that may not be directly related to your circumstances, I have suggested that you contact me. I welcome questions about The Model and related matters.

Enlightening Alignment Summary

Apart from minor organisations, I argue that all organisations can benefit from adopting The P9 Management Model. The degree to which they benefit depends on their ability to (finely) tune the alignment of their six operational elements.

Enlightening Alignment occurs when the knowledge gained from the ten explanatory chapters of The Model, together with applying the content of the following three chapters, becomes successfully applied within your organisation. This chapter delivered answers to questions of practicalities and curiosities. Naturally, there will be more details and discussion on a tailored fitment for anyone committed to adopting The Model.

The chapter also introduced the two words that can form your organisation-wide cohesive mantra: Enlightening Alignment. These two words become a proprietary short code when discussing the improvement of any task or item. They act as a continual focus point or motivational phrase. They are yours to use.

Do you now believe that The P9 Management Model is the *"holistic solution for organisational success"* that I stated would be delivered? Hopefully, you do. However, if you are not entirely convinced yet, the following three chapters, being:

- The P9 Decision-Making Matrix
- The P9 Cohesive Management Culture
- The Summit State

might prove to be the conclusive evidence you need.

12

THE P9 DECISION-MAKING MATRIX

> *"Whenever you see a successful business, someone once made a courageous decision."*
> **Peter F. Drucker**

When the opportunity arises, my sub-30-second elevator pitch consists of one rhetorical question, one unsolicited answer, and my recommended solution (namely, The P9 Management Model).

- The question; ***I have a rhetorical question for you. What is the biggest stumbling block to reaching your organisation's full success potential?***
- My answer; ***I say that it is simply the quality of the daily decisions that you and your management team make!***
- My solution; ***let me introduce you to an alternate management model that empowers you and your team to make decisions that will lead your organisation to sustainable excellence. Here are my contact details.***

Again, like many before me, I have studied numerous books and articles Peter Drucker wrote. I like the above quote for its apparent simplicity and hidden gem; that is how I see it. For a successful business to exist, somebody once decided to create it. That same somebody would have probably faced considerable risk and challenging obstacles; hence Drucker used the word *courageous* to amplify the significance. However, I also see that a business or organisation cannot exist without processing **continual** decisions.

As a senior or (even) a mid-level manager, you have to make decisions every day, and you rarely get all the information you need before making a decision. My experience is that many managers survive by thinking that while they may get numerous decisions wrong, they will all be okay if they are correct when deciding the critical ones. A few managers have suggested they believe many decisions they have had to make resulted in average outcomes (never intentionally). However, when it was crucial to get it right, they put a lot more effort into the process.

Disappointingly, we have all made decisions that we live to regret. With the advantage of hindsight, we would have changed those decisions. We would have made a different decision. However, you don't always get the privilege of not making or delaying a decision.

Again, as a CEO or senior manager, you make decisions daily. Most decisions do not require lengthy analysis; you instinctively know the right decision. Nevertheless, you regularly have to make decisions that will have measurably negative consequences if you make the wrong decision.

So, if you don't currently use decision-making systematic thinking processes, then now is an excellent time to start. Reward yourself and your organisation by utilising a systematic method of *thinking and checking* to maximise the results of making good decisions. Adopt or develop a technique that works for you. Ensure that it is a method that suits:

- Your competency level
- Your behavioural profile
- Your confidence level as a result of consistently good outcomes

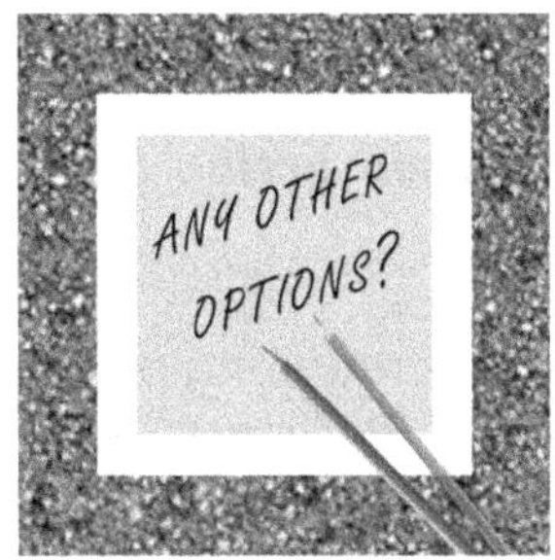

The Model's success and your organisation's success essentially rely upon the quality of your daily decisions and your management team's decisions. This premise is not a pioneering or ground-breaking statement; it's reality. Many highly successful CEOs have developed and honed their methods of effective decision-making. Many have studied decision-making models and often tailored their own by selecting portions of multiple models.

Some of the more well-known models include:

- Administrative Model of Decision-Making
- Analyze the Situation
- Implement the Decision
- OODA Loop
- Paired Comparison Analysis
- Rational Decision-Making Model
- Retrospective Decision-Making Model
- The Ladder of Inference
- Vroom-Yetton-Jago Model

Each of the above models has distinct intent, focus, and methodology, but that list is not extensive. The marketplace offers many more solutions. Do a web browser search for: *'how often do managers have to problem solve?'* You could spend hours reading the raft of theories, models, opinions and tips on becoming a good problem solver. Eventually, any reasonable person will conclude that a good problem solver requires you to be a good decision-maker.

Dictionaries offer numerous definitions for the word *decision*. In my opinion, the most straightforward meaning of a decision is "***a decision is the chosen action from known or unknown choices***".

Every sector has challenges requiring people with the appropriate authority to make crucial decisions daily. A good example is the commercial airline industry which historically has been, and remains, commercially volatile. Each airline company knows that it relies upon its customers having confidence in its prioritised and tangibly apparent commitment to human safety. Naturally, systems and perpetual practical training are vital.

> ***Sideline***: *I have regularly watched the television series Air Crash Investigation. The show's producers use computer-generated imagery to re-enactment the sequence of events that led to each disaster. Some episodes depict a pilot making crucial decisions aware of the potential risk of fatal consequences. In contrast, they show pilots making decisions in other episodes, not knowing their actions could lead to a disaster.*
>
> *I justify watching an episode by assuring myself that there are qualified experts in all the relevant matters of aircraft safety. The producers promote that in the cases of previous fatal incidents, where investigating authorities and the industry learnt better ways of doing things. Consequently, I am confident that every time I (or my family) hop on a commercial aircraft, its chances of arriving safely at its destination are incredibly high.*
>
> *Airlines have developed numerous compulsory checklists for pilots, co-pilots, and flight attendants to complete before leaving a terminal. Once airborne, they must follow highly developed and tested protocols if there is an unwanted safety issue in the cockpit. Every word, task, action, and each decision gets recorded on the flight data and cockpit voice recorders, which are highly robust.*

I'm a great believer in asking questions that require considered answers. When I recall those who have mentored me during my adult life, I realise that the ones who benefited me most were the ones who followed the 80/20 rule; 80% of what they had to say was in the form of questions, with the remaining 20% being direct advice or recommendations. I have certainly applied that 80/20 rule to those whom I have mentored.

I consider that one of the most powerful words in the English language is the word **WHY**; Questions beginning with *why* necessitate more than a one-word answer. Unless outrageous or nonsensical, the *why* questions insist you consider your answer before delivering it. Subject to how intentionally crafted the question was, a higher level of thinking is required.

There is an art to being a good questioner. Of course, anyone can ask a question. Still, not everyone can craft a question that digs deeper without offending. Particularly a question that is not just requiring a fact to be delivered. Instead, it needs the answerer to realise that more questions are probably coming from whatever answer they give; hence they better be sure that their explanation is appropriate. I am not referring to the court-style witness box 'interrogation' questioning, but a style where the answerer knows that the questioner is for them, not against them; the questioner is on their team, wanting them to kick yet another goal.

R.Q. *What are some of the best-crafted questions you ask your C-level managers?* ***W.I.D.***

Questions can stretch your thinking. Questions regularly require you to:

- Think beyond historical procedures; dig deeper into context and reasons

- Consider where you are, how you got there, and whether there could have been an alternative pathway
- Think way outside of the box
- Cause you to imagine future consequences, both positive and negative

This book's fundamental purpose is to equip you, as a CEO or senior manager, with information, knowledge, methodologies, and philosophical approaches. Not providing you with an introduction to the decision-making model that I have developed, used, and shared, would be an injustice.

You make two types of decisions daily; consequential and inconsequential. Naturally, the intent is to make successful decisions, yet logically, the risk of making decisions leading to failure exists. CEOs and other C-Level managers are often positive thinkers, leaning on being confident optimists. However, they also understand risk.

Say you have a *matter* (of practical importance) that requires a decision. C-Level managers could use the essential primary thought filter table that illustrates the possible risk outcomes based on the *Probability of Failure* and the *Consequence of Failure*. I am not sure who to credit for its creation, and I have seen it called both the *Consequence of Failure Matrix* and *Consequence of Failure Table*. For your matter of importance, you can use it to estimate a potential risk by determining the probability of failure and the consequence of failure on a 1 - 5 basis. The cross-reference location cell determines the risk.

Probability of Failure (POF)		Consequence of Failure (COF) 1	2	3	4	5
	1	Very Low	Very Low	Low	Medium	High
	2	Very Low	Low	Medium	High	High
	3	Low	Medium	High	High	Very High
	4	Medium	High	High	Very High	Very High
	5	High	High	Very High	Very High	Very High

It is a simple yet effective high-level overview helpful in identifying a *matter's* level of urgency and deciding the amount of consideration time you will invest.

Nevertheless, as with most models or tools, its accuracy relies on a minimum of two criteria. The suitability of the repeatable method you use in deciding its 1-5 weighting of Probability & Consequence values. Secondly, the quality of the information you use that guides you to the chosen values will determine its accuracy.

The latter depends on the value of the questions you ask to discover the correct information. The questions you ask will be the product of your thought patterns, i.e., how you have trained your brain to think.

> ***Quick Alert:*** *Suppose you are already a proficient questioner who has developed and honed your effective decision-making methods. You have a reputation for wisdom substantiated by a proven track record for the same. In that case, feel free to skip the following and go to the next chapter.*

Retrain your brain to rethink your thinking.

Is the way we think a result of a habit? Are the processes that we use formed out of previous practices? What would be required if we wanted to change our thought process, irrespective of age and experience?

Can you genuinely *Form a New Habit in 21 Days*? I imagine you have heard this claim on numerous occasions; I certainly have. You will find an endless list of books (some by credibly distinguished authors) written on the topic and innumerable bloggers who contribute their opinions. Ironically I could not find any peer-reviewed research data to support the claim. Other articles that I have read suggest it takes 66 days to form a new habit, while yet another proposed 320 days.

However, you can read many papers written by credible psychologists substantiating the practice of retraining your brain to think differently and subsequently form new habits.

The critical factor is motivation, having the desire to change your thinking. Remember, the goal to become exceptional is at stake; to become remarkable, you need to be an excellent decision-maker.

Before I share the process I usually apply when deciding on a crucial work-related matter, I will inform you of a little of my journey that led to this process.

At the end of the last millennium, I spent twenty years in varying sectors: financial services, information technology, and corporate training. For me, workwise, everything was racing, including company expansion, new systems and technologies, changing workplace environments, faster-growing global economies, increasingly competitive markets, and tighter external governance compliance.

There were also numerous corporate collapses and forced merges, while many start-ups also existed. It was an exciting yet challenging season. Consequently, many decisions had to happen promptly, not every time, with all the desired information (available) and opportunity for performing the intended due diligence. Subsequently, errors of judgement led to disappointing outcomes; most were repairable but regrettably, not all.

The greatest lesson I learned from that season was to be better prepared. My two critical areas that needed improvement were due diligence procedures and decision-making, necessitating better processes. Both matters needed one solution, **the right questions**, a light bulb moment! Now you might say it was too obvious. Still, without having a disciplined, systematic approach to knowing what information was essential and how to make the best decision, my experience confirms it was not immediately apparent. And that, right there, is why we all need to retrain our brains to rethink our thinking. My thinking, formed by previous events, procedures, and mind patterns, had me locked into creating conclusions that lacked sufficient detail, evidence, and insufficient consideration of potential consequences.

The next decade majored in observing how other highly successful managers and leaders made good decisions. I wanted to know what was their default pattern of thinking and deciding. I did not wish to (merely) hear their theories. Before taking decisive action, I sought their mental processes, triggers, reactions, responses and final contemplations. I am grateful for those willing to share their recalled experiences with me.

Indeed, having acquired such information and having already created the architectural structure for The Model, I knew that eventually, I would have to write a book that provided every crucial step and component contributing to organisational success.

Once I had crystallised my approach and increasingly gained confidence in the three core and six operational P's of responsibility, I felt empowered to craft and test the appropriate questions. I knew the questions must cover potential issues and opportunities, including many of those highlighted in the Issues List (introduced in the Production Management chapter).

Now to my decision-making approach, which I have based on everything you have so far read in this book. A less determined person could think it complex and unnecessary at a novice glance. In contrast, a P9 Model Graduate would immediately understand its methodology and welcome its value.

Today you and I can have the privilege of looking at a problem, challenge, or opportunity through The Model's filter of structure and philosophies. Through your experience, you know a crucial decision in one area of responsibility can affect one, many or all 9Ps. Therefore, the questions crafted had to consider and comprehensively address all the relational impacts of the 9Ps.

Twenty-four questions form a matrix consisting of two categories and four progressive layers. The two categories are *Generic* and *P9 Elements* specific. Following are all the questions, with explanations where beneficial, grouped in four layers that cover:

- **The Issue** requiring a decision - 12
- **Core Elements** considerations - 6
- **Operational Element specific** considerations – 5
- **Post decision** task - 1

The first two question layers are generic. You may use them to decide on any issue, challenge, or opportunity that comes to you. I recommend that if you begin answering Question 5 (onwards) of The Issue layer (the *Intermediary* section), you should, at a minimum, answer Layer Two *Core Elements* questions.

The Issue Layer

This layer consists of twelve questions divided into two timeline sections.

The sections are:

1. **Primary** (4 initial investigation queries)
2. **Intermediary** (8 essential knowledge findings).

However, answer the four Primary questions, and if your final answer is NO, you are finished. This result is a frequent experience for a senior manager. If your answer to Question 4 is *YES*, proceed to the Intermediary section. You embark on a serious consideration trip if you begin answering the Intermediary questions.

The Issue Layer questions are:

1. ***What is the issue?***

   The subject issue, challenge, or opportunity necessitates clear identification to be worthy of your time. Your Team, customers/clients, or external people will want to discuss all types of matters. Some will be clear to understand, irrespective of their value, while others will speak or write in only vague terms. The latter is often because the matter presented (the subject issue) hasn't yet matured into something easily recognisable or communicable.

2. ***How did it come to my attention? (Chanced upon? Incidental? Motive/Agenda?)***

   This step further clarifies the subject issue by you considering its source. By chance, did you discover, recognise or identify it? If not, was it presented by another person, and, if so, what is their motive or agenda? Knowing this will either fast-track the process and/or provide insight.

3. ***What or who are the key impacted victims/entities of the matter?***

   Even if you consider it a lightweight issue, you might still want to deal with it, depending on *what* or *whom* you think it will impact. Of course, this is only a high-level view.

4. ***Do I think it is worthy of my (consideration) time?***

Your answer may be immediate; otherwise, here is your first opportunity to use a tool to estimate its value, such as the Consequence of Failure table described earlier in this chapter. Your colleagues and other stakeholders consider you valuable. You also value your time, so it must remain high on your priority list. Therefore, your options remain:

- *Investigate further*
- *Ignore*
- *Postpone*
- *Delegate the issue*

5. ***What weight value do I give to the issue?***

1 = very low | 2 = low | 3 = medium | 4 = high | 5 = very high

Every issue has a value, even if you consider that value to be zero. This question is the beginning of lower-level considerations, requiring more detailed analysis. One possibility for giving it a higher value than others might think it worthy of would be if you knew that its fit in the bigger picture merited it.

6. ***What would be the consequences of no action?***

The answer to this question is not necessarily directly linked to the value you previously gave the issue in Question 5. You may be thinking any of the following:

- The impact of the subject issue may be greater than its value
- The value of the subject issue may be greater than its impact
- The perceived lack of interest could cause concern
- There is an immediate consequence of no action
- There is a potential longer-term consequence of no activity on the subject issue

- There is no consequence of not taking any action on the subject issue

7. ***What resources are required to achieve resolution/ solution?***

Initially, this might be only a high-view assessment, and you intend only to complete an evaluation if you proceed with the subject issue. The question's value rests in the estimated total sum of the required resources as a factor in making a decision.

8. ***Who (or possibly What) are the key contributors to the solution of the matter?***

This question goes further than Question 7, in that you are now thinking about:

- Who would need to contribute, and what proportion of their time would need scheduling?
- What teams would need to contribute, and what proportion of their time would require scheduling?

9. ***What will be the desired outcome/product of this matter?***

This answer usually requires you and at least one person from your executive team to agree on what the outcome will look like and deliver. This prediction somewhat crystallises and confirms whatever answer you gave to Question 1. Alternatively, it might identify additional work needed before completion or it might raise other opportunities.

10. ***What are the solution options?***

The person or team leader in your answer to Question 8 is likely to provide at least some, if not most, of the conceived alternate options regarding the subject issue.

11. ***From the list of solution options, what are the recommended choices?***

This question is redundant if Question 10 only produces one solution. Otherwise, this is where your team gets to shine by delivering an expert-founded recommendation. Depending on the predicted Risk of Failure and Consequences of Failure in Question 4, and the value given in Question 5, you might:

- Accept the presented recommendations
- Modify them
- Reject them in preference to an option that considers knowledge unknown to others

12. ***What critical P9 elements' relational factors could have unintended consequences if left unconsidered?***

The answer to this question is often the game-changer between an OK decision and an exceptionally positive one. It presents an opportunity to (again) consider your answers to Questions 5-8 **by first glancing at the bullet-point list of *The 36 Relational Factors of The P9 Management Model*.** It is your penultimate step before making your decision on the subject issue. You filter it through the P9 lens, ensuring that consideration has occurred to all the relevant relational factors of the remaining operational elements.

When you answered Question 11, you had reached the moment where most experienced senior managers were ready to make their decision. Question 12 introduces another paradigm; as a part of the P9 Graduate mindset. It refers to your knowledge of the relational factors of all nine Ps. It presents the opportunity to contemplate the subject issue through your P9 lens.

The Core Elements Layer

While Question 12 of The Issue Level focused your awareness on the P9 relational factors, with the intent that, at a glance, it might bring one or more consequential matters to your attention, it was only a high-level task. The Core Elements Layer goes a level deeper, ensuring that you consider the pertinent intent of each question. Notice that there is only one question for each Operational Element.

This layer, equally divided into three sections, consists of six questions. The premise of these questions reflects you are moving a step closer to a decision while still ensuring you cover the *Core Elements* contingencies.

Purpose Questions

1. ***Does this matter have any critical governance implications?***
2. ***Do current policies already cover this matter, or does it require policy creation/amendment?***

People Questions

3. ***How will we best support those selected to create, improve, or rectify this matter?***
4. ***What are the measurement methods intended for assessing the outcome of this matter?***

Processes Questions

5. ***What, if any, processes and procedures will need amending to achieve this matter's desired outcome/ product?***
6. ***Who needs to be informed of the result of this outcome/product?***

You will experience that the above questions regularly achieve their intent, crafted to prompt your mind to other relevant Core Element-related matters.

The Operational Elements Layer

Together, the previous Question 12 of The Issue Layer and the six questions of The Core Elements Layer are an excellent step up from conventional decision-making procedures. However, if you progress to the third layer, you will have leapt up!

The P9 Decision-Making Matrix has five questions for each Operational Element. Each set of questions, precisely crafted and personalised for the final decision-maker (CEO or senior manager), ensure the subject issue, by now fully identified as relating to a specific Operational Element, addresses the targeted crucial points of concern.

For continuity's sake, the eCommerce component, an example from the Enlightening Alignment chapter, seems appropriate for the third targeted question category. Now is an excellent opportunity for me to explain that the inherent flexibility of The Model allows you to determine what activity areas best relate to which particular Operational Element within your organisation.

Some activity areas would best or automatically fit under the same Operational Element in almost every organisation. Good examples would include:

- Legal Compliance, appearing under the Protection (governance) Element umbrella
- Policy Reviews, appearing under the Policies Element umbrella
- Product Design, appearing under the Production Element umbrella

Others, such as Public Relations, might best fit under the Protection Element umbrella or appear under the Promotion Element umbrella. Of course, specific activity area components may need the consideration of other attributes that alternate Operational Elements offer.

When an organisation's needs necessitate a variance of the standard questions used in this matrix, assistance is available to ensure that the questions drafted are in a manner that is consistent with The Model's philosophies. This flexibility is a foundational strength of The P9 Management Model.

Again, for the sake of consistency (as in examples in previous chapters), let us treat the subject issue as being under the Promotion Element umbrella; then the five questions are:

1. ***Why am I confident that the envisaged promotion related to this matter will comfortably operate under our governance guidelines?***

2. ***Does the foreseen required promotion related to this matter comply with our relevant policies?***
3. ***Will the promotion related to this matter require an altered behaviour or mindset?***
4. ***What measurement system exists (or is required) to determine the successful performance of the marketing/public relations process related to this matter?***
5. ***Regarding this matter, what confidence do I have in our existing practice or policy to ensure that we respond to the market feedback from our promotion?***

I should stress that not all issues, challenges, or opportunities necessitate progressing to Level 3 questions. While I would never describe The Operational Elements Layer as optional, I would prosecute that it is conditional upon the gravity of the subject issue.

One might describe The Operational Elements Layer as icing on the cake, a (distinction) step of wisdom that confirms and enhances your decision.

The Post Decision Layer

This layer consists of just one crucial question.

1. ***Having now decided, what are the detailed notes I need to make to support my decision?***

This final decision-making task is another differentiator between the average organisation and those aiming for sustainable excellence.

By following The P9 Decision Making Matrix with your instincts and sense of correctness, you have every right to be confident that you have invested an appropriate amount of thinking time and due process essential to result in a successful outcome.

You have not taken any unnecessary shortcuts, nor did you rely upon unquantified and unqualified guessing. You performed as a professional CEO or senior manager should. You acted in the best interests of your organisation and yourself. Therefore you have no reasonable cause to be anxious about summarising the explanations for your decision and briefly describing all the procedures you took during (the process of making) your decision.

> ***Quick Alert:*** *If you are already recording detailed support notes for your decision, skip this section and proceed to The P9 Decision-Making Matrix Summary.*

The value of this final task lies not in the 24 questions asked but in the details of your answers. The advantages include the following:

- It offers valuable material for future reflection
- It provides a basis for a proprietary template for future decision-making
- It delivers decision-making training material for current and future junior executives
- It assists in protecting you from inaccurate, unfounded and unreasonable criticism
- It increases the intellectual property value of your organisation

> ***Quick TIP:*** My recommendation is that you create a *decision-made* styled template for recording future decisions and continually improve it to optimise its value and efficiency.

The P9 Decision-Making Matrix Summary

Again, as previously stated, as a CEO or another C-level manager, you are already well experienced in making decisions. I want to be blatantly clear, the success of The P9 Management Model does not rely upon you exclusively using The P9 Decision-Making Matrix.

Nevertheless, as previously stated in this chapter, "*The P9 Management Model's success essentially relies upon the quality of the daily decisions of you and your management team.*" Based on the purpose of The P9 Management Model, the essence of this statement is about organisational success and sustainable excellence. To achieve such, you as a CEO, your executive management team and even your lower-level managers must continually make decisions that optimise positive outcomes.

Hence, I would strongly encourage you to do one of the following:

- Continue to use a decision-making methodology that you are confident is equal to, or better than, The P9 Decision-Making Matrix, or
- Adopt parts of The P9 Decision-Making Matrix to include in whatever model you currently use, or
- Use The P9 Decision Making Matrix

13

THE P9 COHESIVE MANAGEMENT CULTURE

> *"Never doubt that a small group of thoughtful, committed people can change the world. Indeed. It is the only thing that ever has."*
> **Margaret Mead**, *American cultural anthropologist*

You are now into the third major part of this book on the journey to organisational success. The first part thoroughly explained the architectural structure, philosophies and user methods of The Model. It took a while to get there, but you endured and arrived at the next waypoint; The P9 Decision-Making Matrix. It challenged you to *retrain your brain to rethink your thinking*. Together, these two parts were essential equipment for you to progress to this waypoint. They have provided you with crucial tools to apply at your discretion and determination.

You have got it all together, and you consider you are good to go! You are ready to apply this newfound knowledge together with your experience to propel you forward. You now have the essential ingredients, so what could hold you back from transforming your organisation into the realm of the exceptional? **Your workplace culture, that's what!** A workplace culture rarely neutralizes an organisation's performance; it either enhances or weakens it. It works for you or against you.

In the book's Preface, I committed to *"help you to develop an organisational-wide culture that will become the envy of your competitors"*. Your organisation will never reach sustainable excellence with a culture that tolerates identifiable limitations. You can have a worthy & defined purpose, remarkably talented people, and highly refined processes for producing great products or services. Yet, the organisation will not reach its whole and desired potential without a culture that works for you.

I have observed that you cannot escape culture unless (I imagine) you find yourself alone on a deserted island. The easiest way to experience a different workplace culture is to move to another workplace, but that is not you. You are a transformational technician, a change manager. If the workplace culture needs amending, you will have the solution.

What is workplace culture? I like the description that the behavioural and data scientist, activist and writer Dr Pragya Agarwal gives, *"Culture is the environment that surrounds us all the time. A workplace culture is the shared values, belief systems, attitudes and the set of assumptions that people in a workplace share."*[42]

42 Dr Pragya Agarwal | Culture - https://www.forbes.com/sites/pragyaagarwaleurope/2018/08/29/how-to-create-a-positive-work-place-culture/?sh=b34928f42727

The culture of your organisation's workforce reflects the culture of your organisation's management. You have probably visited organisations where there is not one workplace culture but multiple cultures; I know I have on many occasions. This reality is typical in an organisation with departmental silos. Naturally, you would expect differing atmospheres in different areas of your operation, but a common culture can still exist; the desired culture.

The P9 Cohesive Management Culture (P9 Culture) *could* be your desired culture. Having read and considered it, I hope you will say, *"The P9 Cohesive Management Culture should be my desired culture"*.

I like the Cambridge Dictionary's five-word definition for *Cohesive*: ***united and working together effectively***[43]. Indeed that is what you would seek for your organisation, true? I encourage CEOs to adopt those five words as a targeted declaration of cohesive power, being inseparable from their executive management team. Fortunately, for which we are all grateful, fewer organisations (particularly in the private sector) still experience attitudes representing *"it's not my problem, I'm certainly not responsible for it"*. Nevertheless, few organisations know the complete number of empowering steps to (radically) improve their workplace culture.

The P9 Cohesive Management Culture introduces a daily practice not yet raised in this book, called ***P9 Time***. P9 Time will be crucial in creating the desired culture while dramatically improving your organisation's performance. As an executive team member, you work harder and longer than most of your staff. Your time is precious.

Yet, you encounter issues that interrupt, irritate, or negatively impact your or your team's day. Some will be directly under your control; they are in your area of responsibility. You can fix them. Other issues that affect your day, caused by an area under someone else's responsibility, are equally irritating. Either way, an issue that negatively impacts your organisation **limits your** work-life satisfaction level, hard-earned current and future rewards,

---

43 Cohesive | Cambridge Dictonary - https://dictionary.cambridge.org/dictionary/english/cohesive

and possibly your reputation. Thus, *someone's problem becomes everyone's problem until solved.*

R.Q. *What is an issue that currently interrupts, irritates, or negatively impacts you or your team's day?* ***W.I.D.***

This new daily practice requires you to invest (just) 9 minutes every workday, typically less than 1.5% of an executive's average workday. It requires your (total) focus on tuning your organisation to become recognised, respected, and rewarded for achieving sustainable excellence! P9 Time: *the nine-minute workday habitual ritual*. More about P9 Time later in this chapter.

The P9 Cohesive Management Culture consists of five components, each beginning with the letter **C**. You will note a trend again allied to the *Keep It Simple* principle. All five **C** components, aligned to The Model's **People Element**, are critical to achieving The Model's desired organisation-wide culture. Before the introductory phase begins, it requires you, as a CEO, to be fully on board and committed to the new cultural style. This culture requires a top-down approach to even begin its pathway to success.

The introductory phase of The P9 Cohesive Management Culture is aimed solely at your **C-level** executive team. Again, the aim is to get senior managers to fully understand and enthusiastically embrace The Model and ensure their organisation succeeds. You will witness success when your (entire) team believes it is a shared responsibility. All C-level managers must first practice it before modelling it. Remember, this is a top-down cultural *Cohesive* practice. It is reasonable then for their mid-level managers to want to see evidence of it working for them before they begin to model it to others.

You also should know that a cyclical rule exists for the P9 Culture. Suppose you move to the second component (Communication). In that case, each following **C** component is a compulsive inclusion, as is their relative position, because each **C** component progressively contributes to the successful cycle of the P9 Culture.

The first component of The P9 Cohesive Management Culture is ***Confirmation***; to be precise, it is *issue Confirmation*. This component begins within your area of responsibility.

Confirmation

This first step conveniently applies the four *Primary* investigation questions of *The Issue Layer* in The P9 Decision-Making Matrix, with a slightly different focus. For expediency's sake, here they are again, suitably amended:

1. ***What is the issue?***

   The subject issue (*issue Confirmation*) necessitates clear identification to be worthy of your P9 Time. Your Team, customers/clients, or external people will want to discuss all types of matters. Some will be clear to understand, irrespective of their value, while others will speak or write in only vague terms. The latter is often because the presented matter hasn't matured into something easily recognisable or communicable.

2. ***How did it come to my attention?*** *(Chanced upon? Incidental? Motive/Agenda?)*

   This question further clarifies the subject issue by you considering its source. By chance, did you discover, recognise or identify it? If not, was it presented by another person, and, if so, what is their motive or agenda? Knowing this will either fast-track the process or provide insight.

3. ***Who or what are the key impacted victims of the matter?***

   Even if you consider it a lightweight issue, you might still want to deal with it, depending on *what* or *whom* you think it will impact.

4. ***Do I think it is worthy of my P9 Time?***

   Your answer may be immediate; otherwise, it is your first opportunity to use a tool to estimate its value, such as the failure table described earlier. However, an organisation committed to being a P9-styled entity aiming to be exceptional, as opposed to your average organisation, always seeks to eliminate counter-productive flaws (in people, processes, procedures, policies, or products and services).

Usually, such identified deficiencies are within your organisation. Still, other flaws may exist in your trading partners and joint-venture partners [e.g. supply chains or distribution channels]). So, you will now find yourself getting involved with issues previously you may have thought unnecessary, trivial, inconvenient, or too complicated. Due to the value your colleagues and all other stakeholders place on you, your time management must remain high on your priority list. Will you investigate it further, ignore, postpone, or delegate the issue?

Of course, even at this point, you will dismiss some issues presented to you as trivial or motivated by a wrong attitude (or agenda). Nevertheless, if you become aware of something that negatively impacts you, your team, or your organisation's performance, it should go on your list of identified items.

The second component is Communication (within your direct and indirect areas of responsibility).

Communication

Issue Communication should be a perpetually present activity within your organisation and highly valued. If you have determined that the subject issue is not a matter to be addressed, at this point, then inform the person who raised it in a manner that does not offend them.

Alternately, say you have identified an issue that needs fixing or further exploration; it may still need quantification or qualifying. Also, remember that the matter may not necessarily interrupt, irritate, or negatively impact your organisation but rather present a beneficial opportunity.

With whom you need to communicate is conditional upon where the area of responsibility lies. Discuss the subject issue with relevant team members if it is (directly) within your control. Otherwise, talk to the appropriate peer manager to discover whether they are aware of the matter and are already addressing it. The latter requires inter-department transparent communication. However, ensure that you do not raise suspicion of an inappropriate plan or unwarranted criticism. Instead, make it evident that you are a colleague who, when necessary, regularly demonstrates their firm commitment to assisting all departments. The primary intent remains to enhance your organisation's culture.

A good starting point is explaining how the issue impacts your team. Often, the manager responsible will not be aware that you or your team are experiencing such frustrations. The communication also needs to be appropriately consistent throughout the timeline of the process, to inform, update, and avoid misunderstandings or task gaps.

The third component is Cooperation, which is apparent and compelling.

Cooperation

Let me make this very clear. You and I know that there are different levels of cooperation; non-cooperative, reluctant, hesitant, passive, minimal, active and total. The P9 Cohesive Management Culture relies on your commitment to active cooperation being consistent, functional and comprehensive; naturally, this applies equally to your peers.

When your team members observe your approach to them raising an issue, it achieves various advantages, including the following:

- That you not only received their raising of an issue, but you are also now proactively addressing it in a manner that demonstrates authentic commitment; this further assists in them raising future issues, as well as again proving that you value them
- That you are serious about achieving a good outcome
- That you are willing to sacrifice some of (or reprioritise) your time and efforts

- That you willingly model what you reasonably expect others to contribute

The fourth component is Contribution, the end proof of commitment.

Contribution

In a P9 Cohesive Management Culture, this crucial component is another differentiator. In many organisations, issues that interrupt, irritate or produce a negative impact can continue because the response is limited to complaining and criticising.

Naturally, if the issue is directly within your area of responsibility, you and your team are exclusively responsible for whatever contribution is required. However, your offer to contribute should be clear and practical to those responsible when it is not your direct territory. The required contribution could include:

- Brainstorming for solutions
- Technical assistance
- Some short-term lending of your team members to work directly on the issue
- Provide them with an introduction to someone within your network of contacts who could help

> **R.Q.** *What additional modes of cooperation would you welcome from your peers?* ***W.I.D.***

The fifth and final component is Celebration, the tangible, expressive acknowledgement and gratitude to all involved in achieving success.

Celebration

Harbhajan Singh is a cricketer and cricket commentator who said, *"Be so happy that when others look at you, they become happy too."*

The nature of the celebration is determined by the gravity of the now resolved issue. The issue may have ranged from a minor problem that only required a brief *high-five* response with the team members accredited with resolving it to a significant event reflecting the value and the substantial benefit of the once troubling, now fixed, issue.

Be careful not to perform an overkill of celebrations. I once observed a small-sized company that I thought would celebrate the opening of an envelope; I exaggerate, but you get my point. You seek to build and maintain a high-performance organisation that regularly exceeds expectations. You do not applaud mediocrity because that undervalues the purpose of celebration. However, you appreciate the benefits of acknowledging and honouring a worthy accomplishment.

The crucial point here is to acknowledge the success appropriately. Some organisations are masters of *celebration management*, while others fail miserably. Become a *'masters of celebration'* organisation. Every time you celebrate reinforces that your team is a can-do crew.

P9 Time

You are an individual who has succeeded, now in a C-Level role. P9 Time is adaptable and tailored to suit your style and behavioural profile. Make it yours; make it work for you. My preference is to have a templated plan. A plan that others grow comfortable with and have confidence in it working. It provides familiarity, structure and an opportunity for further strategies.

It is not a social gathering. It is intentionally highly focused and time-limited, which I prefer to divide into two sections. Five minutes to identify an issue, confirm its worth, and form an initial action plan - four minutes for updates on previously raised issues. Occasionally, you resolve an issue within the four minutes provided, but typically, it introduces a newbie. It is not a talkfest. Its intent is clear; tangibly progressing your organisation towards sustainable excellence.

Three of the P9 Culture's five 'C's, Communication, Cooperation and Contribution, occur outside P9 Time. Successful outcomes of Confirmed issues range from days to months, conditional on the resources required, logistics, and people factors.

The P9 Cohesive Management Culture Summary

P9 Time is a crucial element in achieving your P9 Cohesive Management Culture. Again I stress that it begins with the CEO, then all other C-Level managers, then Mid-Level. In your organisation, you might decide your team supervisors should practice it. You can imagine how many matters that otherwise remain tolerated or ignored get addressed because of P9 Time. Consequently, the culture changes due to the regularity of visible practical performance improvements; your people see themselves as once a 'we can-do it' crew to (now) believing they are the '***WE DO DO IT***' team.

> ***Quick Alert:*** I must point out that there is considerably more to The P9 Cohesive Management Culture than I have included in this chapter. My intent in providing this chapter's selected content was to focus on the easily achievable matters that produce the highest returns. Other crucial and beneficial matters essential to building a preferred culture tend to be sector or organisation specific. Such matters require direct discussion, which I am always willing to accommodate.

So summing up, the following is what you can expect to experience after implementing The P9 Cohesive Management Culture into your organisation.

You will see the evidence in radically diminishing complaints and criticisms. The *blame game* gets replaced by the *same game*; proof that your team is saying *we are all on the same team, we are all in.* All of them identify negative issues, irrespective of their origin; all work together to resolve them.

It will continue with declarations including;

- We are *Cohesive*: *united and working together effectively*
- We value one another at all levels of responsibility
- We believe in our organisation's Core Values Declaration
- We will not tolerate mediocrity or slackness on our team
- We work smart and celebrate hard
- We are changing and improving our communities
- What we do matters, so we matter

That is what your P9 Cohesive Management Culture-styled organisation can be like!

R.Q. *What items are on your priority list for your organisation's future workplace culture?* ***W.I.D.***

14

THE SUMMIT STATE

> *"Perfection is not attainable, but if we chase perfection, we can catch excellence."*
> ***Vince Lombardi***, NFL Coach

The meaningful intent of this topic's title will become more apparent to you in the next few minutes of reading.

Wow, you have arrived. Superb, seriously. I recognise and acknowledge you as a person of persistence and commitment. You have now finished absorbing all the extra technical details that I believe are essential for top-shelf organisational performance. You have a game-changing management model that introduces a new paradigm for senior management to transform your organisation. You are empowered to achieve and optimise the number of successful outcomes from the copious decisions made daily by yourself and your executive managers. Throughout this book, I frequently presented word imageries of what your organisation could look like in the future. To top all that, you now have a real-world practical approach to developing an envious organisation-wide cohesive culture.

As a CEO, the buck always stops with you. I am here to say that YOU can do it. With a bit of help, you can master everything I have presented. You and your team can begin the transformational change required for your organisation to become exceptional. With what I have given you, together with employing all other established, proven, prudent, and professional practices, your organisation could become a sector leader. You could become the CEO of an exceptional entity.

Nevertheless, my desire remains for you to go further as a CEO. In the Introduction, I declared: *Simply put, I am an advocate for sustainable organisational excellence.*

Merriam-Webster defines ***sustained***[44] as: ***maintained at length without interruption or weakening***, and the word ***excel***[45] is described as ***to be distinguishable by superiority: surpass others***.

Sustained excellence never occurs overnight; its timeline measurement unit is decades, not years. Organisations that achieve *sustained excellence* have one common denominator; exceptionally superior leadership.

History proves that many examples of bright and capably experienced CEOs are appointed to improve a company's performance; dramatically and with rewards that reflect the size of such improvement. Sadly, you and I know numerous financial levers can adjust a company's Profit & Loss Statement (Statement of Financial Performance). While achieving the short-term objective of increased net profits over 2-4 years, some of those lever movements also cause a weakened Balance Sheet (Statement of Financial Position). I am sure you can easily name the ones immediately coming to mind.

I do not believe that the above-described management style is (in any way) honourably exceptional. Some observers and commentators have seen it as clever, but most stakeholders were disadvantaged. I hope there will be many new or budding

---

44 Sustained definition| Merriam Webster - https://www.merriam-webster.com/dictionary/sustained

45 Excel definition | Merriam Webster - https://www.merriam-webster.com/dictionary/excel

CEOs among my readers who want to become P9 Management graduates. In this case, I deliberately elevate leadership over management as the primary goal. Yes, to a degree, every manager must lead, but there is a distinct difference between them and popularly acknowledged leaders of substance.

However, I'm a realist. I know that two types of hope exist, *baseless* and *qualified*. *Baseless* hope has little or no reasonableness. In contrast, having read the structure, principles and philosophies delivered in this book, I hope you now believe it qualifies you to achieve the intent of this book and further it inspires you to apply it.

I aim to see you develop and live by your *'personal'* purpose. Indeed in the first **Core Element of the Purpose** chapter, I stated, *"I have learnt that Purpose can be an excellent guide to making personal life-changing decisions. Purpose can influence your behaviour while also influencing the behaviour of others. Purpose can also shape your goals by offering a clean and clear sense of direction."*

Exceptional leaders don't just happen; they develop. They are men and women who are determined to be their best selves. They purpose to be honourable; they start by desiring to be principled and live up to that.

So, here's the thing, because you have arrived on this page, I can now accept that you are genuinely earnest about management. Yet, sustainable excellence is a quantum step up from notable management; it requires remarkable leadership. In this book, while I may have occasionally mentioned leadership, my primary focus, till now, was always on delivering quality input that would assist you in becoming an exceptional manager capable of introducing and overseeing the transformational change described.

Still, a repeatably noteworthy leader has qualities unrelated to physicality, qualifications or work-life experience. The qualities I refer to are internal, primarily matters of the mind and heart.

To arise and become a remarkable leader, you need to answer a critical question honestly, with a hand on your heart.

Are you the best you possible?

The question is intrusive but not deliberately judgemental, at least in this case, not from anyone other than you. Years ago, having been requested to write a sentence of twenty words or less that I solemnly believed summed up who I was, I meditated on it for days. Eventually, I wrote this: *I'm a human being trying to be better than my yesterdays and preferring to see the potential in people.*

R.Q. *If asked, What would you have written that sums up who you are? W.I.D.*

I can only speculate that you must have kept reading this entire book to gain knowledge of transformational change within your organisation. You have achieved a bucket load of knowledge, but are you prepared? You may be ready to perform the CEO's expected (demanded) role, but are you prepared to lead a sustainably excellent entity?

Quick Alert: *If you are already the best you, feel free to move on to the next and last chapter.*

Are you the best you? No one else can wholly answer this question. Conditional upon your circumstances, your partner, children, siblings, parents, and closest friends may have valid perspectives, but they don't live inside you. They don't know all the things you think about or even what you do when isolated from them; sometimes, the things you think and do restrict you from being your best.

We all have flaws, some of us more than others, and those who disagree are immediately flawed. Can you identify any personal transformational changes essential for leading that organisation to sustainable excellence?

Like most people, I dare say there are things about my life that I would not have chosen, starting with physical proportions and attributes. Mainly, they are things that I can not change. In contrast, there are a few things that I didn't like about myself that I have been able to change. My temper is one example. It was not outrageous but evident, never violent or intentionally aimed at others; instead, I would become frustrated, verbally abusive, and angry at myself. Still, others present could be intimidated. I did not acknowledge it was a significant problem in decades past, even when raised by those close to me. Fortunately, I reached an age where I cared less about admitting my flaws and more about being transparently authentic. The temper has not yet wholly vanished but is now considerably milder and rarely exposed. Also, I have had to work on my character determinedly; not yet perfect but distinctly improved.

And right there is the beginning of wisdom; *"God, grant me the serenity to accept the things I cannot change, courage to change the things I can, and wisdom to know the difference."*[46] A desire to change introduces options.

I believe we are all on a journey through life that presents us with countless personal options. For me, these were options including:

- How I communicate
- How I think
- My love language
- What I think about
- What is my default response to a problem

46 The Serenity Prayer | written by the American theologian Reinhold Niebuhr (1892–1971)

- What triggers my more profound feelings of frustration
- What my core beliefs are
- What is my default response to an opportunity
- What makes me react
- How I view and value other people
- How I view and evaluate myself
- The non-negotiables in my life
- My loyalties
- My reliability
- My honesty
- My ability to forgive (myself and others) and within what typical timelines
- What and who I trust
- My anxiety levels and causes
- My level of self-confidence
- My propensity to criticise
- My tendency to procrastinate
- My ability to make essentially necessary decisions that will disadvantage multiple people
- My level of concern about my popularity
- Currently, what is my dream future
- The price that I am prepared to pay (or will not pay) to achieve my ambitions

I call them options because it is a list I have had to consider and, where necessary, take action to improve. It was constantly confronting, but I knew I had choices to make each time I faced an undesired matter. The above twenty-five examples are all self-assessments. Still, asking those close to you will produce benefits too. Their input will either confirm or challenge your perceptions.

You must know that you cannot expect to lead a highly successful organisation long term if you (by choice) carry personal inadequacies.

Did any of the above items raise more than a bit of concern for you? If so, go into action and put a strategic change-management plan together to rectify them. You don't have to settle for less.

Now that you understand the principles and the resulting value of The Model's P9 Time, and, if you do not already, favour yourself by spending a few minutes (maybe 5) a day working on personal improvement. Set aside a couple of minutes to meditate and reflect on your personal goals, then set out the subsequent tasks necessary for reaching the best you. It is amazing what one can achieve when there is a laser-like focus on a step-by-step improvement plan.

Your people want to be led but don't want to be led poorly. As a manager, you may have good skillsets to do the job, but do you possess the character and integrity to lead exceptionally? I want to encourage you and, if necessary and requested, guide you to become the best you possible.

I make no apology; that is who I am. I have been an organisational performance consultant for decades while concurrently being an executive or senior pastor in local churches. My faith and church (community) leadership experience do not qualify me to tell you what to do, but I hope it helps you understand what motivates me to encourage you. I do not intend to use this book to evangelise and indeed not to proselytize; that is not me. Nevertheless, to better explain my moral and philosophical compass, I try to follow this biblical instruction: *"To act justly and to love mercy and to walk humbly"* (Micah 6:8). **Justice**, the receiving & giving of **mercy** (forgiveness), and **humility**; are three worthy objectives.

Whatever your philosophical compass looks like, I hope it directs you to *be your best you;* because an outstanding leader needs some cornerstone foundations that build character and successful longevity.

There are many self-improvement solutions that I would like to share with you if ever the opportunity arises, but for now, here are just four valuable tips for your consideration.

Don't suffer from situational amnesia.

This topic may not be you. Still, it is good content for you to use with your team when the need arises.

I have listened to several CEOs speak from their office chair or boardroom suite, a restaurant table, at conferences, seminars, podcasts, or in the offices of professional external advisors such as their lawyers or accountants. I occasionally recognised that their recollection of a matter or situation (known to me) was (at best) inaccurate or, worse, a known untruth. The circumstances of a particular situation were either exaggerated, understated, or misrepresented.

My approach, when applicable, has not been limited to just identifying their motive; instead, I attempt to discuss it with them and identify the root cause. Whenever I have had the opportunity to coach or mentor someone, I accepted the responsibility of *calling them out* when something counter-productive to their character arose. Never publically, of course.

Most people can stretch the truth when telling a yarn, a joke, or describing the size of a fish caught. However, that is not what I am referring to here. You must know the sort of things I am describing, the ones that matter. There is also a scale of frequency to consider. When observed by those you lead, even the infrequent little white lie can result in their uneasiness — the more frequent, the more their cautious apprehension develops until the increased regularity causes it to blossom into constant mistrust. Once respect is lost, you will find yourself on a slippery downhill slide, from which you can hardly ever reverse.

Rarely is the person performing this behaviour unaware of doing it. Usually, they simply do not consider or appreciate the ramifications. My point is, do not let that be you. My encouragement to you is this; if you identify any tendency to do the above, talk it through with someone you trust to be confidential, wise and absolutely in your corner. Identify the triggers, and pre-prepare some alteration actions.

Even those who inspire need inspiration.

Exceptional leaders inspire others, especially those they lead. Inspiring others is not the core curriculum of any university degree I am aware of, nor do I see any consultants offering money-back guarantees for promising to inspire you. An inspiring leader is not just the result of an acquired skill set; it results from many qualities, including transparent character, wisdom, courage, and ceaseless integrity.

Sometimes, you will motivate your people, stretch them, challenge them, or even frustrate them; each impact might be intentional, depending on particular circumstances. However, you cannot intentionally inspire; either you are inspiring, or you're just not.

You could be an inspiring leader if, presuming firstly, you apply this book's contents. Secondly, you do not intend to remain in ownership of any character inadequacies by choice, and finally, *you actively work on being your best you*. I summarise the last two sentences in three words: *Knowledge, Wisdom* and *Professionalism*.

If you discover you are inspiring (Btw, congratulations), you will still benefit from consistently developing the habit of seeking and receiving inspiration from others. I have learnt that certain things that inspire me do not necessarily inspire everyone else and vice versa. Nevertheless, keep drinking from the wells of your inspiration sources.

Remain on mission.

The more success you experience as a CEO, the more competing distractions arise. You will become financially secure, affording you to acquire many of the material things you desire. This ability is a good thing. You deserve personal rewards and the capacity to create a comfortable environment for those you love.

You will also gain a reputation for being notably successful, placing more demand on your time. People will want and expect you to share your journey experiences by speaking at seminars, conferences, events, media interviews, and panels.

People, known and (mostly) unknown to you, will offer countless opportunities for personal gain. Invitations to numerous significant events; sporting, adventure, entertainment, charitable, and political. More invitations will occur, including board positions on industry bodies, sporting, community and environmental organisations. You are also likely to spend more time with consultants and advisors specialising in Public Relations, media grooming and profile management.

Due to your higher profile, your organisation will increasingly experience more offers and ocassional opportunities for mergers, takeovers, alliance partnerships, and sponsorships.

The above can be advantageous if managed well, with strategic objectives and predetermined boundaries. However, if not tightly controlled, performance and reputation can erode quickly.

Forbes, Wired, The Economist, Harvard Business Review, and Bloomberg BusinessWeek are notable for their journalistic contributions to the business world. More than ocassionally, in each, you can read articles that directly or indirectly mention a CEO, previously recognised for being exceptional, is now considered a *has-been.*

I encourage you to remain humble and regularly reflect on the daily tasks, dashboard priorities, areas of focus, practices and behaviour that made you succeed. If you can stay motivated and committed, with a strong belief that you are still the best leader, your organisation needs you. Otherwise, it's time to transit to another organisation or retire. I never criticise a CEO who believes their time is up, particularly if they want to retire and spend more time with their family.

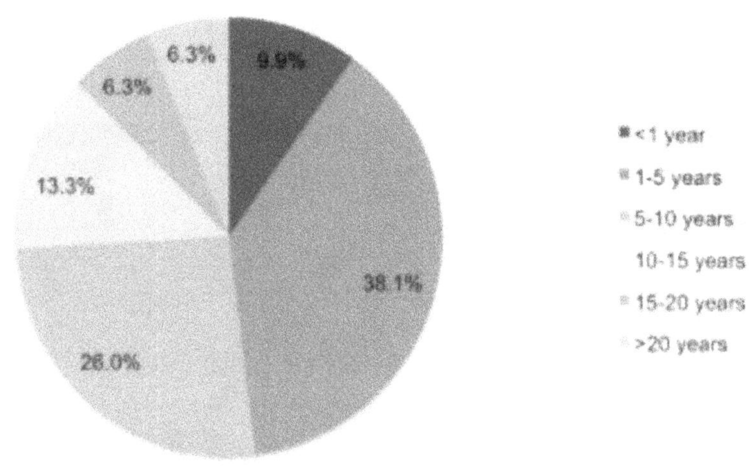

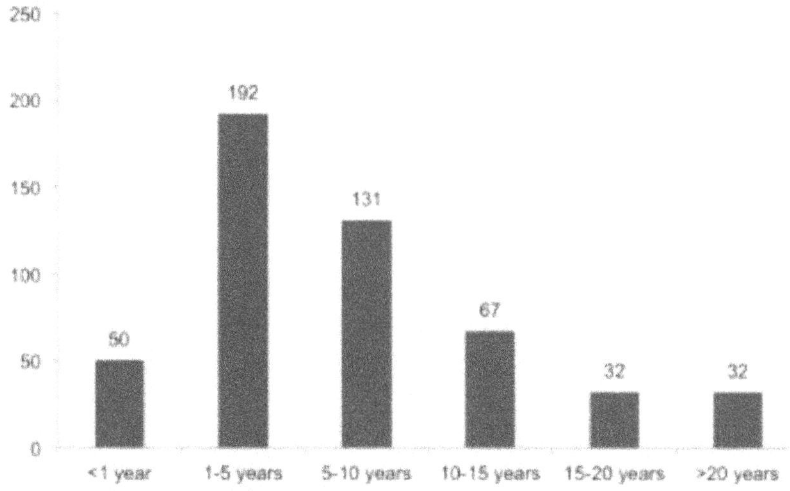

However, in decades past, I regularly pondered the trend of the decreasing CEOs' tenure. I understand the various arguments promoting the upside of an organisation having a fresh set of eyes at the helm. I also appreciate CEOs wanting to have diversity and multiple examples of improving bottom lines. I invite you to read a well-researched Harvard Law School Forum on Corporate Governance article by Dan Marcec[47], Director of Content & Communications at Equilar, Inc., titled CEO Tenure Rates. See the graphs.

> ***Sideline:*** *Is every large-cap organisation an example of sustained excellence? Large-Cap organisations do many things well, but there are various roads to becoming a leading capital entity, including monopolisation, patent management, and early niche entrance. Nevertheless, several Large-Cap corporations have met their demise within my working career by being anything but excellent. Cap value alone is no guarantee of longevity.*

Based on the 2018 data above and more recent research, the exciting news is that fifty per cent of CEOs have been there for more than five years. Say you are privileged to have transformed an organisation from its average past to becoming exceptionally good. Say you do not identify another individual who will (genuinely) do the role better than you; then, it is not in your organisation's broader stakeholders' best interests to leave unless you retire.

Pass it on.

As a highly successful CEO, your contribution is of substantial value to your community and nation. You have acquired much; experience, knowledge, perspective, hindsight and wisdom. You also have developed a significant network of professional and community leaders. You have influence.

Irrespective of your age, as a CEO, if you rise to the exceptional sphere, I would argue that you are obliged to pass on those abovementioned attributes to the individuals you have cause to believe will one day be a respected CEO.

47 CEO Tenure Rates | Corporate Law - Dan Marcec - https://corpgov.law.harvard.edu/2018/02/12/ceo-tenure-rates/

Earlier in this chapter, I stated, "*Sustained excellence never occurs overnight*". Nor do CEOs become exceptional within a couple of or even a few years. Apart from the essential competencies, capabilities and capacity to do the job, proteges require nurturing, not babysitting or micromanaging, but mentoring. This responsibility requires a medium-term commitment and an often inconvenient investment of your time.

Sometimes you will discover an individual rising star and want to fast-track their rise. By all means, please include them in you're A-Team mentoring program. However, my recommendation is to apply the *input & test* approach. Over time, consider giving them a set of tasks or projects that will stretch their weak areas. They are on your A-Team because of their strengths and victories. Still, you know that your concentrated effort to improve your weak spots and the ocassional failure to excel helped prepare you for your role. Horticulturists advise that *"times of pruning aren't fun, but they are essential"*. Eventually, your tests became your testimony! It will be experiencing these stretching tasks and projects that will either elevate them further or identify unforeseen outcomes.

I encourage you to create a legacy of being a widely acknowledged developer of proteges who excelled. Pass It On!

The Summit State Summary

Hopefully, you now get this topic's title, which refers to an organisation that has attained and maintained sustainable excellence. While such organisations are slowly growing in number, they remain far too few.

Today, more than ever since the beginning of the Industrial Revolution, organisations that excel do so by gathering intelligent, capable and skilled individuals who, as senior executives, cohesively manage exceptionally. Nevertheless, alone they cannot succeed. They need a leader, an exemplary individual who knows that you will not reach sustainable excellence by taking shortcuts, tolerating sub-superior standards (relating to processes or people) or underperformance in any P9 area of responsibility.

Above are just four helpful tips that I recommend you consider. Of course, one should not view them as mutually exclusive or collectively exhaustive. Still, I remain conscious of two points of commitment I made in the Preface:

- *"Finally, this book is not an exclusive academic work. Instead, it is* ***an informal management guidebook.****"*
- *"I desire to share critical organisational success factors without turning the book into Tolstoy's War and Peace."*

Other topics are also essential to organisational success that I have not included in this book, for example, Board Engagement and External Stakeholders. With appropriate qualifications and experience, numerous authors have written worthy books with insightful and practical advice on these topics. I hold strong opinions on several relevant matters that I have not included. These topics require explicit content and a narrow focus, maybe for future books.

Still, those four tips, if followed, will produce remarkable results. They represent a philosophical approach that I have observed several quality CEOs successfully apply.

15

YOUR FUTURE PATHWAYS

> *"The vast possibilities of our great future will become realities only if we make ourselves responsible for that future."*
>
> **Gifford Pinchot** - first head of the United States Forest Service and the 28th governor of Pennsylvania.

So, this is where the rubber finally meets the road. You have now equipped yourself with extraordinarily effective management tools and philosophies. You have acquired yet another asset in your set of professional tools. The few hours spent reading this book, meditating on its points raised, and making a few notes along the way, if applied, may prove to be the best professional development course you have undertaken to date.

Irrespective of whether it was your intention, the contents of this book will impact your thinking and influence your future. Indeed it will influence the future of those around you.

The future of your community and beyond lies extensively in the number of CEOs wholeheartedly committed to leading highly successful organisations desiring sustainable excellence. The result of you reading this book is that you now have the responsibility of making a crucial decision regarding your and your organisation's future.

That last paragraph may seem a little dramatic. It is nevertheless the reality. Ultimately, your future depends on what you consider to be the available options. Subsequently, your choices will result from those options.

Following are several possible pathways forward:

- Go live as if you had never read the book (*Please let this not be you)*
- Choose to (independently) apply certain aspects contained in the book
- Choose an exploratory discussion (with me) on a specific topic or a broader subject
- Choose to request I assist with a few preliminary tailored P9 surveys to assess your organisation's strengths, weaknesses, needs, and opportunities
- Request I assist you in using The P9 Excellence Index, thereby creating your organisation's current 'excellence value' as a baseline reference point against future Index measures
- Book a place in The P9 Management Academy's Master Classes to begin your journey to becoming a P9 Management Graduate
- Consider becoming a P9 Platnum Group Client. Contact me to discuss

Scenarios and Recommended Solutions

To add additional value for you, as a future exceptional leader that has read this entire book, consider if one of the following scenarios applies to you.

Scenario 1 | The Start-Up

You are an entrepreneur. You are about to become the CEO (possessing the complete authority of management control) of an exciting start-up organisation, anticipated (based on matters that confirm your confidence) to be a medium-sized enterprise within five years. As I stated in my Introduction, *"if undertaking a start-up, the contents will be an excellent roadmap to strategically fulfilling your objectives."*

You are fortunate. You have the opportunity to design, craft, develop and implement your plans using the entire contents of this book. You will not experience many, if any, of the common obstacles experienced by CEOs of established organisations. Your challenges will lie elsewhere. Indeed, your greatest challenge will be time management.

If so, start with and prioritise the basics.

- Determine the purpose of your organisation, remembering the key points about Organisational Purpose outlined in the Purpose chapter. Please write it down in a Purpose Statement
- Write your organisation's Vision Statement and its Mission Statement. Even if you do not publicly present them, these benefit you and your future organisation
- Consider, meditate on, and determine what core values your organisation will adopt and practice. Then, write your Core Values Statement
- As I stated in the People chapter, *"I believe CEOs should write their own Workplace Culture Statement."* Envision your organisation's look and atmospheric feel, then write your Workplace Culture Statement
- Declare from the beginning that your new entity is a P9 Management Model organisation, and then share with your key recruits the inherent benefits of that

- Contact me to assess what further assistance, particularly in strategic planning matters, is immediately available

Scenario 2 | Future CEO

You have mapped out your future. You have reasonable cause to believe that you are only a season away from being offered a CEO role. You might already be a C-Level manager. You are not yet in complete control, but you have almost total managerial autonomy over your area of responsibility. You have personal buy-in to The P9 Management Model. You want to adopt its methods, principles, and philosophies as much as possible within the constraints of your organisation's policies and current leadership.

If so, here are some recommendations.

- Commit to becoming the best you before you finally take on the CEO role. Ocassionally reread the previous chapter, The Summit State, and allow its contents to influence any area of your life that you consider is restricting you from being your best. You will never be perfect; none of us can be. Nevertheless, it is likely you can significantly improve your current best. Becoming the next exceptional CEO always starts with you.
- Reread The P9 Cohesive Management Culture chapter and allow it to consume your thinking about how you see the future of your current area of responsibility.
- Think long and hard about your desired department's look and atmospheric feel, then write your department's Workplace Culture Statement. Then, please share it with your trusted key managers and share its concept origin. If deemed appropriate, seek their input, and should that prove beneficial, add to or edit your Workplace Culture Statement. The more that buy-in, the faster the results.
- Introduce the P9 Time approach to your key managers. A well-introduced, well-led and well-applied daily P9 Time will considerably improve your department's performance.

- Consider joining The P9 Management Academy's Master Classes to begin your journey to becoming a P9 Management Graduate.
- Allow your department's improved results to speak for themselves. Encourage your team to take the credit; they will know where it came from, and as a result, they will publically credit you.
- When the right occasion arises, and you are confident about how the recipient will respond, share The P9 Management Model with your CEO. Your department's results and your team's respect for you should be sufficient to receive an appreciative and welcomed response from a CEO that has not previously been aware of The Model.

Scenario 3 | Current CEO

You want to achieve change! You have heard the Wake-Up call, and when it comes to The P9 Management Model, you are all in. You agree with the principles, methods and philosophies of The Model. The contents of my book have inspired you. You want to be the next exceptional CEO and lead an organisation widely known for its sustainable excellence.

If so, chuck a 'Nike' and just do it!

- Begin by investing some time in noting your ambitions, goals, and expectations. Ensure you note the beneficiaries of perceived future accomplishments.
- Revisit the purpose of your organisation. If your organisation's Purpose Statement does not exist, work with your board to write one, remembering to address the critical points about Organisational Purpose. Develop and write a statement that, if genuinely reflected by your transparently evident commitment and daily practices, your Executive Management Team will become willing to do almost anything to see it through to fruition. If you need assistance, contact me.
- Review and use 'Anderson's The Change Leaders Roadmap Diagram' to plan how you will proceed.

- Consider joining The P9 Management Academy's CEO Master Classes (with separate sessions only available to qualifying CEOs) to begin your journey to becoming a P9 Management Graduate.
- To maximise and accelerate your and your organisation's full potential, consider becoming a P9 Platnum Group Client. Contact me to discuss.

Scenario 4 | Previous CEO

You still want to influence. You have been there, experienced it, and know what is real. Whatever your reason, you have read this book and liked its content. You are not looking for fame. You don't need more money. But like me, you want to see more organisations become high-performing entities obtaining sustainable excellence. Beyond your knowledge, experience and success, you have a vast network of valuable contacts whose experience and skill sets differ from yours. You have invaluable opinions, thoughts and ideas. You don't have time to mentor one-on-one, but you still want to contribute.

If so,

- Consider having an exploratory conversation (with me) on a specific topic or a broader subject
- Let me know if you think I, my readers, or clients should be aware of something you have written or produced that could benefit the cause

Your Future Pathways Summary

Abraham Lincoln once said, "*You cannot escape the responsibility of tomorrow by evading it today.*"

In the opening paragraphs of this chapter, I advocated, "*The future of your community and beyond lies extensively in the number of CEOs wholeheartedly committed to leading highly successful organisations desiring sustainable excellence.*"

Now I would like to finish by prosecuting my firm belief that your future potential does not belong to you alone, nor does it belong to only your organisation. You are becoming a highly developed, specialised, increasingly valuable and finely tuned weapon against organisational performance mediocrity. Surely you realise that not fulfilling your full potential will cause a regrettably measurable loss of significance to your community and beyond. I do not wish to offend, and yes, I am passionate about this cause; as I warned you in the book's Preface, *"I have a passion for successful organisations and an ongoing desire to share my knowledge and experience."*

I sincerely hope that whatever number of healthy and capable years I have left on this earth will be productive. I desire to bring a significant number of equally passionate and more knowledgable and capable women and men on this journey to sustainable excellence within an ever-growing cohort of inspiring and high-performing organisations.

Finally, irrespective of your location, occasionally mentioned throughout this book was my offer to assist you, and it was a genuine offer. Whether it is a simple enquiry or a specific matter of need, please send me a quick note at my email address, and I will respond ASAP.

16

THE AUTHOR'S FINAL THOUGHTS

> *"Success is not final, failure is not fatal: it is the courage to continue that counts.*
> ***Winston Churchill***

Note: This chapter is a bonus gift; some random thoughts I did not explicitly include or develop in the previous contents. They are not compulsory reading.

----------oo00oo----------

The following question best introduces another topic I didn't fully cover in this book: *As a CEO, do you prefer to be a Polyculturist or a Monoculturist?* If you are unfamiliar with agricultural terms, Polyculture describes where more than one crop is grown simultaneously in the same space. It is the alternative to Monoculture. Monoculture, the cultivation of a single crop in a given area, is widely used in industrial and organic farming and has increased efficiency in planting and harvest.

My point for raising this topic is best delivered in another two questions: Where is your focus? How many pathways are you attempting to manage? You may think that the previous chapter's *Stay on mission* section dealt with *'focus'*, and you would be correct. However, that section majored in personal focus, whereas now I am referring to your organisation's direction. I regularly say the following phrase: *Think big by taking The Big View, but always with one eye on the rear vision mirror.* Your organisation may produce multiple products or services, yet it should always retain a defined order and remain aligned with its Purpose Statement. Two areas that require caution, particularly in an entity experiencing exponential growth, are takeovers and globalisation. Again, these topics deserve considerable understanding and attention to ensure that those core factors that created your success, are neither diluted nor ignored. I always recommend you attain specialist advice regarding these matters. As you may suspect, I have gathered many due diligence questions (and have developed some myself) concerning these crucial matters, including contingent issues that cover capacities (financial, logistical, and people), competencies (qualified and quantified), and strategies. Again I state that if you have a need and a desire to be helped, I genuinely want to assist you.

Occasionally, I am asked about the value of an MBA. Or specifically, *Do I need an MBA?* My answer is usually conditional upon their answer to my responsive question (did I mention that I am a perpetual questioner): *What do you believe you would do better if you attained an MBA from a credible university?*

There are various reasons individuals undertake a Master of Business Administration degree, or particularly an MBAE, including:

- Some feel obliged (even pressured) to *tick that box* as part of their career plan
- Some arrive at a non-CEO C-Level role from a narrow career pathway; they consider it beneficial and personally essential if they are ever to be considered for the CEO position
- Some because they know their destiny is in the CEO's office
- Some, like me, because they were, or were soon to be, consultants to C-Level executives

- A few because they are perpetual students

Investing your time and (also for most) your money into an MBA programme requires a significant commitment. You may want to ask yourself, is this the right season to begin the program? Should I complete an alternative Master's Degree in a discipline that would have a more direct and immediate positive career result?

If you decide to undertake an MBA, then here are a few tips I recommend you consider:

- Do your homework before choosing a university
    - Look beyond the name
    - Look at their MBA promotion
    - Consider their MBA program slogan
    - Assess their primary marketing points
    - Do these align with your values?
    - What optional units do they provide?
    - What workplace or (optional) international experiences do they offer?
    - Does their timetable work with yours?
    - Does the location work for you?
    - Does their delivery mode work for you?
    - Check out their relevant faculty's history
    - Can you identify each professor or lecturer for each unit?
    - Research each professor's or lecturer's experience. Ensure you are comfortable with the outcomes
    - Use LinkedIn or your broader network of contacts to identify individuals who have done their MBA with that particular university. Reach out to them to discover their assessment of the university and the relevant faculty

- Before beginning the journey, determine your expectations and then ensure you review these regularly throughout the journey
- Determine to create good relationships with your cohort. They may become valuable long-term professional contacts or, even better, become your friends

I think an MBA's principal value is gaining a broad and deep understanding of what a CEO will experience and how it assists in one's preparation for the role.

Among Fortune 100 companies in 2019, 54% of CEOs held a graduate degree, and 59% were MBAs. Nearly forty per cent of Fortune 500 CEOs have an MBA on their resume. Nevertheless, that equates to sixty per cent of Fortune 500 CEOs not having an MBA.

The bottom line to these stats is that the bigger the organisation (by capitalisation), the more likely the CEO will have an MBA. If you consider starting an MBA, I encourage you to know and feel comfortable with your reason.

I have long been aware that not every CEO or budding CEO buys into The P9 Management Model and its philosophies. Yet I live comfortably with that reality. Some see it as too simplistic, others as unattainable idealogy or insufficiently proven. *"Whether You Think You Can, or Think You Can't... You're Right"* is a famous quote by Henry Ford. It is what you believe that counts. Passionately, I think what I share in this book will significantly assist its target audience.

Also, one crucial thing that the decades have taught me is not to become overreactive to criticism and rejection. I value this quote: *"A ship doesn't sink because of the water around it; the ship sinks because water gets in and overwhelms it."* (author unknown). We all get the choice to determine our mind's diet. I choose not to consume negativity, unsolicited counsel, or unreasonable or inaccurate criticism. That does not mean I don't hear it. Instead, using the above *ship* analogy, I promptly plug it and move on. In contrast, I occasionally seek a critique on a specific matter from a select number of people I respect for their wisdom.

The world has now been living with COVID-19 for a few years, resulting in a tragic global death rate, and further, those who will suffer from significant long-term medical issues. Many other challenges have confronted organisations, including having many people working from their homes. Mostly, management and their teams have faired well.

Still, under unusual pressure loads, some mid-level and even the occasional C-Level manager have revisited the territory and practises of a micro-manager. I raise this topic only for you, as a CEO, to consistently keep in check. We live in a world continually evolving its industrial relations and workplace practices. People are looking for and expecting more freedom.

The Model empowers you, your management team, and your people to excel in their current roles. You have attracted and trained the right people, their positions are well designed and specified, and you have refined your processes and procedures, so let them get on with it. From a productivity perspective, better to fix the odd mistake than to suffer the consequences of having your whole team conscious of being continually monitored without cause.

Your life matters. You matter to family and friends. You matter to your organisation. You matter to your community. At the same time, every human life is preciously valuable, although the reality is that the loss of some lives impacts their communities more than others.

Why am I getting all philosophical on you? I'm not. If anything, I am coming from an actuarial viewpoint. The bottom line here, you are valuable. Your family and employer might benefit somewhat from separate life cover policies, but your extinction will have numerous consequences beyond sadness.

So, I strongly encourage you to remain fit and healthy, physically, mentally, emotionally and socially. The total sum of this book's described success and achievements is insufficient should those closest to you prematurely lose you. Whatever you like to do to keep physically fit, do it, and don't stop doing it. Whatever you need to do to remain mentally stable, take the time to do it. Whatever is required to maintain your emotional balance, take the time to achieve it. Stay in touch with close friends and past colleagues; they are also essential to your well-being.

Professional privacy and discretion are high on my value list. I am always disappointed when an individual possessing a professional or commercial relationship with an organisation shares information that a reasonable person would consider intellectual property or Commercial In Confidence. I am sure the organisation they are referring to would prefer they cease and not repeat such behaviour.

I choose not to promote or discuss the clients I work with, who they are, or other proprietary details. I might speak about a sector I am working with or an issue I am working on without disclosing the entity, even if such discretion costs me some business opportunities.

I always look forward to meeting a prospective client, specifically when referred by an existing and satisfied client. Ocassionally, when asked for suggestions on explaining The Model, I recommend they gift their contact with a copy of the book.

As you now appreciate, The P9 Management Model is a holistic and sophisticated approach to management and leadership. One major objective and motivation for writing the book came from the time it takes to explain The Model thoroughly.

Also, the targeted readers represent a relatively small niche. Consuming time explaining The Model to a manager who is not seriously committed to exceptional management and sustainable excellence is merely unwise. Even after a prospective client shows genuine interest, I still recommend they read the book for the following two reasons:

1. To gain knowledge of both The Model's structure and philosophies
2. To provide them with a future reference manual to reconsider a specific topic when they can't recall its details

Well, you have finished reading the intended contents of this, my first book. In the Authors Preface, I expressed the following: *"I wrote this book to assist senior managers (or up and comers) who, like me, have a passion for the pursuit of excellence within their organisation. I have written this book hoping to inspire you to excel and join the limited number of renowned and rewarded executives leading organisations that contribute to transforming their communities, nations, and beyond."*

I am eager to hear your response to those words and hopefully discover that you willingly responded, *"Yes, I'm all in. I want to excel. I want to become a P9 Graduate and transform my current (or future) organisation. I want to experience it and earn a reputation for sustainable excellence."*

Suppose that describes you, having read the whole book and appreciated its contribution to your future as an exceptional change manager and inspiring leader of a widely respected high-performance organisation. In that case, again, I state that I genuinely want to assist you. The book's contents are the introduction to the next level. Wherever possible, I will work with you in a mutually suitable manner. Prepare to become an outlier, statistically. An individual that will not cope with ordinary, average, good or above average. Someone that is consistently abnormal and counter-culture, breaking new ground and reaching altitudes that few CEOs even dream of, let alone seriously attempt.

----------oo0oo----------

Now seems like an opportune moment to ask a favour from you. What was your initial reason for reading this book? It would be fantastic if you took a couple of minutes to send me a brief note also expressing why you purchased the book and what has been your experience having read my book.

Further, and for the last time, I would love to discover that you now desire to become a P9 Management Model Graduate, a CEO committed to leading their organisation towards sustainable excellence.

----------oo0oo----------

That's enough for now.

Oh, just one last question.

R.Q. *Will You Become The Next Exceptional CEO?* ***W.I.D.***

I wish you well.

HOW CAN WE HELP?
TELL US
WHAT YOU
ARE THINKING.

If you want to ...

> Bulk order the book

> Contact the Author

> Schedule Russell to speak at your event

> Schedule a call to Russell

Contact us

enquiries@managingexcellence.com.au

ABOUT THE AUTHOR

Russell Driscoll is a management advisor specializing specifically in organisational performance and transformational change.

His skillsets come from decades of management experience and business equities, including participation in automotive engineering, real estate, financial services, retail, hospitality, technology, and management consulting. His consulting years have enabled him access to many other sectors.

Among his consulting pursuits was a need for a tool that would accelerate the timeline of senior managers to go from good to exceptional. Indeed having completed his MBA, he finally completed the development of The P9 Management Model.

Many of Russell's insights come from his parallel career as an ordained pastor in Christian ministry.

Russell is a husband, a proud father and grandfather.

READER'S NOTES

www.ingramcontent.com/pod-product-compliance
Lightning Source LLC
Chambersburg PA
CBHW061147220326
41599CB00025B/4383

* 9 7 8 0 6 4 5 5 5 3 5 1 2 *